LOST
FUTURES

Owen Hopkins

The
Disappearing
Architecture
of Post-War
Britain

LOST
FUTURES

Royal
Academy
of Arts

First published on the occasion
of the display 'Futures Found:
The Real and Imagined Cityscapes
of Post-War Britain'

Royal Academy of Arts, London
18 February – 29 May 2017

Exhibition catalogue
Royal Academy Publications
Beatrice Gullström
Alison Hissey
Carola Krueger
Natalie Kulenicz
Peter Sawbridge
Nick Tite

Project editors: Tom Neville
and Vicky Wilson
Design: Jon Kielty
Typeset in Neue Haas Grotesk,
Swift and Space Mono

Colour origination: Gomer Press
Printed in Wales by Gomer Press

British Library Cataloguing-in-
Publication Data
A catalogue record for this book
is available from the British Library
ISBN 978-1-910350-62-1

Illustrations
Cover and pages 28–29: detail
of Tricorn Shopping Centre,
Portsmouth, photographed by
Sam Lambert (see pages 68–71)
Page 2: detail of Queen Elizabeth
Square, Glasgow, photographed
by Henk Snoek (see pages 42–45)
Pages 6–7: detail of Trinity Square,
Gateshead, photographed by
Sam Lambert (see pages 82–83)

Thanks to Valeria Carullo,
Catherine Croft, Kate Goodwin,
Helen Ikla and Jonathan Makepeace
for their help in realising this project.
Owen Hopkins

Contents

Ambition and Ideals:
The Changing Fortunes
of Post-War British
Architecture, 1945–2017

Just before 6 o'clock on the morning of 16 May 1968, Ivy Hodge, a 56-year-old cake decorator, went to the kitchen of her flat on the eighteenth floor of Ronan Point in Newham, east London, to make a cup of tea. Leaning over her cooker, she lit a match. An explosion ripped through the kitchen, blowing apart the concrete panels that formed its outer walls and causing the entire corner of the 22-storey building to collapse like a house of cards. Miraculously, Hodge herself survived, having been thrown across the room, but four people lost their lives and others were injured. Had the explosion not occurred so early in the morning, more fatalities would have been inevitable.

Reaction was swift: the building was evacuated, with residents accommodated in a nearby school; Home Secretary James Callaghan visited the site to see the damage, demanding an immediate report on the cause of the collapse; and the press turned their attention to the tower block's construction. Later investigations would reveal that the joints holding the large load-bearing concrete panels together were not strong enough to withstand even a modest explosion; Ivy Hodge had, after all, survived. New building regulations would ensure that the structural defects of Ronan Point would never be allowed elsewhere – but in hindsight the catastrophe can be seen as a watershed moment in post-war British architecture.

In symbolic terms, the closest equivalent to the Ronan Point disaster was the demolition of the Pruitt-Igoe housing estate in St Louis, Missouri, in 1972 – only twenty years after its completion – hailed by the critic Charles Jencks as the moment when 'modern architecture died'.[1] In Britain, however, things were rather less clear-cut. When Ronan Point collapsed, the tide had already begun to turn against high-rise towers and vast housing estates, with several architects exploring low-rise solutions that were more familiar to potential residents.[2] Nevertheless in the 1970s, the perceived and real failures at Ronan Point and elsewhere proved pivotal to a general and decisive loss of faith in the ability of architects – and modern architecture – to build a better world. In time, the very idea of the future as something to be strived towards would come under attack and many of the buildings that were designed to help bring it into existence would be demolished. In varying parts familiar, surprising, acrimonious and salutary, these are the stories this book tells.

It is sometimes forgotten that Ronan Point was repaired and remained occupied for another eighteen years before its demolition in 1986 and replacement by traditional semi-detached houses. By this time, modern architecture was under sustained assault. Prince Charles had just delivered his 'monstrous carbuncle' speech in which he lambasted modern architecture in front of a stunned audience of members of the Royal Institute of British Architects (RIBA).[3] Meanwhile, Postmodernism was in full swing, its ironic historicism and alignment with big business and the market appearing to be at distinct odds with the social agenda and lofty ideals of Modernism. But away from questions of architectural taste and philosophy, of far more lasting significance were the housing policies of Margaret Thatcher's Conservative government. In 1980, early in her premiership, Thatcher moved to end the council-house building programmes that had so fundamentally changed the British urban landscape and introduced 'right to buy', which allowed council tenants to buy their homes at steep discounts. From that point on, the role of the state in housing provision – and much else besides, as Thatcher unveiled her government's transformative economic agenda – would be greatly diminished.

During the 1980s, 1990s and into the 2000s, the sight of post-war housing blocks being brought down became a familiar one across the country. As the demolition contractors' explosives initiated synchronised ballets of rubble and dust, cheers would frequently go up from the crowds of spectators, some of whom had actually called home the buildings whose destruction they were celebrating. Although housing drew the most ire, it was far from the only building type that was subject to the wrecking ball. Schools, libraries, public buildings, even factories, which a generation or two before had been designed and built as expressions of collective or civic values, were derided as concrete monstrosities to be razed from the face of the earth.

More recently, post-war architecture has undergone something of a rehabilitation, and in some quarters it has become unmistakably fashionable – a remarkable turnaround. Buildings such as the Brutalist Preston Bus Station by Building Design Partnership (1968–69), at real risk of demolition less than a decade ago, are now protected by listing. At the same time, a proposal to include the live demolition of several towers from Glasgow's Red Road Flats (designed by Sam Bunton & Associates, 1964–69) as part of the 2014 Commonwealth Games opening ceremony was widely seen as insensitive and disrespectful, though in the 1990s it might have been welcomed as an emblem of the city's regeneration. The towers still came down, of course, surviving another year before their date with destiny. Despite this change, in south-east England and especially in London, the rate of destruction of post-war buildings is probably greater than ever, as commercial buildings reach the end of their useful lives and rising residential prices make the redevelopment of so-called failed and low-density inner-city

Vacant and boarded-up flats at Robin Hood Gardens, Poplar, London (Alison and Peter Smithson, 1972), await demolition.

housing estates ever more attractive. No amount of campaigning from post-war architecture enthusiasts and social-housing advocates has, for example, managed to save Alison and Peter Smithson's Robin Hood Gardens in Poplar, east London, a Brutalist housing development completed in 1972 and revered by architects internationally.

While many people have come to admire Britain's post-war architecture, the views of many more have remained the same – or even hardened. In January 2016, then Prime Minister David Cameron announced a £140 million fund to demolish around one hundred 'sink estates'. In a reprise of arguments from the 1980s, Cameron equated concrete Modernist architecture with crime and social deprivation: 'In the worst estates ... you're confronted by concrete slabs dropped from on high, brutal high-rise towers and dark alleyways that are a gift to criminals and drug dealers'.[4] It did not take much analysis of the numbers involved (coupled with the fact that the £140 million turned out to be a loan) to see that this was a wholly political statement – intended to reassure the Conservative Party's traditional voters that the government was on their side – rather than a realistic proposal. Cameron and his advisers were no doubt fully aware that given the value of the sites occupied by many housing estates, particularly those in inner London, redevelopment is all but inevitable, even without their intervention.

Despite continuing protests, demolition began on the huge Aylesbury Estate, Walworth, London (Hans Peter 'Felix' Trenton for London Borough of Southwark, 1970), in 2012.

Proposals of this sort, in a broader context of the erosion of social housing through both the continuation of the 'right to buy' policy and the often rather lopsided partnerships between local authorities and developers, have naturally provoked strident criticism from the political left. For some, the 'decanting' of council tenants from an estate, its demolition and subsequent redevelopment for private sale is tantamount to a kind of social cleansing of the poor from Britain's cities. As a result, protests and pressure groups have sprung up around many estates whose future is seen to be under threat from regeneration.[5]

One effect of the polarisation of the debate has been to distort the way we see post-war architecture. This book aims, as far as possible, to take a balanced view, providing a dispassionate record of 35 buildings across a range of types constructed from 1945 to 1979 that have been – or are very shortly going to be – demolished or heavily altered. It is intended neither as attack nor as lament, but rather as an exploration of the ideas and values that shaped the creation of these buildings – and how changing external contexts, whether social, economic or political, as well as their own internal characteristics, have played a part in their destruction. It provides a vivid illustration of the way architecture that was conceived to bring about a bold new future was lost along the way.

Brave new world

As soon as air raids began in autumn 1939, it was clear that, whatever the outcome, the country that emerged from the Second World War would be very different to the one that had entered it. That said, those early raids could hardly have suggested the unprecedented destruction of Britain's cities during the height of the Blitz in 1940 and 1941, with Liverpool, Bristol, Cardiff, Manchester, Portsmouth, Southampton, Coventry, London and many more hit countless times. Despite the pressing need to resist invasion and, ultimately, to defeat Nazi Germany, thought was also given to what sort of country might emerge from the destruction.

In 1941, William Beveridge, a liberal economist, was commissioned by the government to produce a wide-ranging report into how Britain might be rebuilt – physically, but also socially and economically. In his report, published in 1942, Beveridge identified five 'Giant Evils' of 'Want, Disease, Ignorance, Squalor and Idleness' and recommended a system of social security to eradicate them.[6] The Beveridge Report, as it is universally known, met with widespread approval and formed the basis of many of the policies implemented by Clement Attlee's government after the Labour Party's landslide victory in the 1945 general election.

Between 1945 and 1951, Attlee's government enacted perhaps the most transformative political programme Britain has ever seen, establishing a welfare state that would provide social security for everyone from 'the cradle to the grave'. Under the National Insurance Act of 1946, everyone in work paid a flat-rate contribution in return for unemployment and sickness benefits and a pension after retirement. In 1948 the National Health Service was established – publicly funded and free at the point of use. The Education Act, which was actually passed by the Conservative-led coalition government in 1944, created a state-funded system that guaranteed every child free education up to and including secondary school. The first comprehensive school, which did not distinguish between pupils according to academic attainment, opened in 1948, but it was not until the 1960s and Harold Wilson's Labour government that they became widespread, superseding the grammar school and secondary-modern system. Steel and coal industries, railways and telecommunications were all nationalised, and full employment became government policy.

To deal with the acute housing shortage brought about by the war, and the already squalid conditions of many city centres, substantial planning reforms were introduced. An Act of Parliament of 1946 paved the way for the creation of a string of new towns on greenfield sites outside major cities and conurbations. Although inspired by the Garden City movement and its early manifestations at Letchworth and Welwyn Garden City, these New Towns were explicitly modern in their architecture and planning. Local authorities were empowered to build on a vast scale, with the aim of providing high-quality housing at affordable rents.

Constrained by material shortages and the economic situation, Attlee and Aneurin Bevan, his Minister for Health, whose remit extended to housing, failed to meet their highly ambitious targets for new homes. Thus for many people, the first taste of the new architectural world was the 1951 Festival of Britain. Conceived to mark the hundredth anniversary of the Great Exhibition and to celebrate Britain's cultural, industrial and architectural future, the Festival was a fillip to national morale at a time of austerity.[7] Exhibitions and festivals took place all over the country, but the main site was on the south bank of the Thames opposite Charing Cross Station. Here, under the direction of Hugh Casson, a series of bold modern buildings was erected to contain the exhibitions. The largest were the Dome of Discovery by Ralph Tubbs; the Royal Festival Hall by Robert Matthew, Leslie Martin and Peter Moro; and the Skylon, not a building as such, but a cigar-

Poster featuring a model of the Festival of Britain site on London's South Bank, produced by the Bureau of Current Affairs in 1951.

The Lansbury Estate, Poplar, London (Frederick Gibberd and others, from 1951), was the focus of the 'Live Architecture Exhibition' as part of the Festival of Britain.

shaped, spaceship-like steel structure, designed by Hidalgo Moya, Philip Powell and Felix Samuely, which was suspended vertically as if about to be launched into the sky. A popular joke at the time was that the Skylon had 'no visible means of support' – like the British economy.

For most visitors, this was the first time they had experienced modern architecture, which had struggled to gain much of a foothold in Britain before the war. The Festival's architecture, with its bold yet approachable Scandinavian-inspired Modernism, pointed towards a better future, as much as anything the buildings contained. It was partly through an awareness or anticipation of this that the Festival's organisers conceived a 'Live Architecture Exhibition' focused on the new Lansbury Estate in Poplar, east London.[8] There, visitors were able to see how modern architecture and planning principles could create a new community and decent homes that people would be proud to live in. It was no doubt something of a disappointment to its organisers that the exhibition attracted only 90,000 visitors and received mixed reviews in the architectural press.

By contrast, for the 8.5 million visitors to the main site, the experience was a revelation, reaffirming national pride and creating widespread optimism about the exciting new future that was just around the corner. However, the reaction from architects was mixed. In the eyes of the influential couple, Alison and Peter Smithson, the Festival was a betrayal of the values of modern architecture. They saw its brand of Modernism as too safe and too sanitised, a far cry from the rougher and more polemical architecture they were exploring, soon to be christened the 'New Brutalism'.[9] By contrast, Richard Rogers, later Peter Smithson's student at the Architectural Association, who visited the Festival as an eighteen-year-old, remembered it as the first time the world burst into colour after the grey drabness of the immediate post-war years.

Reactions

In autumn 1951, Attlee's government lost the general election to the Conservative Party under Winston Churchill. Despite the popular success of the Festival of Britain, many on the political right viewed it as little more than socialist propaganda. Soon after returning to office, Churchill had the Festival buildings torn down and the site cleared, leaving only the Festival Hall as a built reminder of that moment of popular optimism.

This can be seen as the first instance of post-war architecture coming under attack for the values it was perceived to hold. For the Conservatives, the Festival buildings embodied an ideology of collectivism and state planning that was completely at odds with their own ideas about Britain's future. Moreover, the symbolism of the site's position, just across the river from the heart of government in Westminster, had surely not escaped people's attention. These were far from 'failed buildings'; the problem was actually that they had succeeded – and the only element to survive, the Royal Festival Hall, would become one of London's best-loved buildings.

Despite this early and notable example of the ideologically driven destruction of post-war architecture, many of the buildings demolished over subsequent decades have been lost for mundane reasons, quite often related to deficiencies in the structures themselves. In the face of urgent need and stringent economic constraints, many post-war buildings were designed to be put up cheaply and quickly. Housing in particular became something of a political arms race during the 1950s as Labour and Conservative politicians tried to outdo one another in how many homes they could build. Under the Conservative Housing Minister Harold Macmillan, public-sector housing completions exceeded 300,000 in 1953 – a number not achieved before or since. The trade-off was often a decline in the quality of both design and construction.

Many problems were the result of industrialised construction and 'system build', in which standardised components are prefabricated and then brought on-site for quick assembly. While it can be very successful, when used primarily to cut costs 'system build' often results in bland, repetitive schemes. In addition, because the technology was not always ready for large-scale employment, leaks and other environmental problems were endemic. Similar issues afflicted many of the glazing systems used in post-war buildings, which were unable to cope with the fluctuating temperatures that large areas of glass inevitably produced. The problems were so bad at James Stirling's History Faculty and Library in Cambridge (1963–68) that the university seriously considered demolition in the 1980s.

As post-war buildings have entered their fourth or fifth decades, many have been knocked down rather than expensively renovated. There is little in this phenomenon that is unique or particular to post-war architecture; it is the life-cycle most buildings go through. The relatively high number of buildings from the 1950s and 1960s demolished in recent years is at least partly a consequence of the post-war construction boom – many have simply reached the end of their lives at around the same time. The scale and pace of redevelopment in London and south-east England has also had an effect. Some observers, particularly on the left, view this as ideologically driven, as one economic system seeking to obliterate the remnants and reminders of another. But looking at the situation in purely practical terms, there seems to be no particular reason, even if the economic system had remained the same, why these buildings would not be replaced once they had ceased to be useful. Indeed, if the post-war moment was about anything, it was about 'progress'.

It is, however, in the very idea of 'progress' – and whether what was being realised in its name was in fact for the better – that we might begin to trace the first stirrings of the reaction against post-war architecture and planning. It was the architectural press that first questioned how far lofty ideals were being matched by the built reality. The most prominent of these critics was Ian Nairn, an idiosyncratic journalist and TV presenter who made his name in 1955 with a special edition of *Architectural Review* entitled 'Outrage', in which he railed against the failures of modern planning. Rather than a bright new future, for Nairn planning had created what he called 'Subtopia': an 'annihilation of the site, the steamrollering of all individuality of place to one uniform and mediocre pattern'.[10]

He had a point. Post-war planners' attempts at improvement had in fact harmed many cities. The old city centre of Birmingham was largely redeveloped and encircled by a noose-like ring road. Similar plans had been drawn up for Glasgow, though there planners settled for driving a motorway through the heart of the city. Attempts were made to replace much of Neoclassical Newcastle, and even Georgian Bath and London's Covent Garden were in planners' sights.[11]

The reaction against modern planning was not confined to Britain. In the US, Jane Jacobs's seminal work *The Death and Life of Great American Cities* (1961) argued against the rationalist planning that separated uses – and communities – exemplified in the work of New York City planner Robert Moses, and in favour of urban heterogeneity and the rights of the pedestrian over the car. Even architects became critical of what was being carried out in the name of 'progress' and 'modernity'. In a 1980s TV programme, James Stirling discussed the post-war changes to Glasgow and Liverpool, the cities he grew up in, and described how, 'The lethal combination is not so much the architect, the lethal combination is the town planner, and the local council and the idea of progress'.[12]

New economic order
By the 1970s, faith in the idea of progress towards a better future, which had fed the optimism of the 1950s and 1960s, was rapidly subsiding. The oil crisis of 1973 had exposed the shaky foundations of the British economy.[13] Britain was no

Front cover of Ian Nairn's 'Outrage', a special edition of *Architectural Review* published in June 1955. The illustration is by Nairn's fellow campaigner Gordon Cullen (1914–1994).

longer the industrial power it had been – and that some still thought it to be. This mismatch between perception and reality had already been exemplified at the Festival of Britain, where a steam locomotive was exhibited while other countries were unrolling diesel and electrified railways.

As the decade went on, industrial relations soured and strikes became commonplace. In 1974, a 'Three-Day Week' was introduced by Conservative Prime Minister Edward Heath in order to conserve electricity – miners' strikes meant that coal for power generation was in short supply. Inflation soared and economic growth stagnated, leading to the coining of a new phrase, 'stagflation'. In 1976, Labour Prime Minister James Callaghan was forced to go to the International Monetary Fund for an emergency loan. Mounting industrial action over wage disputes saw the country all but grind to a halt during the 'Winter of Discontent' of 1978–79. Rubbish went uncollected, bodies were left unburied and petrol stations closed as tanker drivers refused to deliver fuel.

Something had to give. In 1979, the Conservative Party under Margaret Thatcher was elected on a radical economic agenda. The next few years would see the unions taken on and ultimately beaten, taxes cut, a massive programme of privatisation of state-owned industries and assets, deregulation of the City of London and the financial-services sector, and major reforms in housing policy. Thatcher decisively rejected the interventionist Keynesian economic policies that had held sway since 1945, and instead followed small-state, free-market principles advocated by economists such as Friedrich Hayek.[14] The result was a new economic and social order, with the collective aspirations of the post-war years giving way to a new era of the individual.

As a highly visible embodiment of the previous era's public values, architecture was soon under assault. One of the most persuasive attacks was that contained in *Utopia on Trial* (1985), a report by Alice Coleman, then Professor of Geography at King's College, London, in which she suggested that design features of post-war housing estates – elevated walkways, multiple storeys, communal spaces – played an active role in incubating crime and antisocial behaviour such as littering and vandalism. Coleman's work provided the ideal academic cover for the dismantling of council-house building programmes and the introduction of 'right to buy', which was intended to turn Britain into a property-owning democracy.[15]

In this political climate, Modernist forms and socialist ideals became almost interchangeable – each representative of the other. Critics of modern architecture became more and more strident in their attacks, opening up space for advocates of traditional styles to make a case for alternatives.

Prince Charles's influence was at its zenith, as a kind of old England neo-vernacular was held up as a true reflection of public taste – which had been trampled on by arrogant and elitist architects. This attitude was exemplified by Kingsley Amis in 'Sod the Public – A Consumer's Guide', an article published in *The Spectator* in 1985.[16] For Amis, architects were among the chief culprits 'of annoyances perpetrated on the public by those who should be serving us ... They have the unique power of sodding the consumer at a distance, not just if he lives or works in the building concerned, or just when he passes it a couple of times a day, but also when he happens to catch sight of it miles away on the skyline'. For many of those on the political right, the equation was simple: concrete buildings were ugly, un-English and made people poor, reflecting a still largely Victorian view of the moral effect of architecture.[17]

Rather less reactionary were the criticisms implied in the work of writers such as J. G. Ballard, whose work became known for its preoccupation with the psychological and social effects of post-war landscapes. Ballard's *High-Rise* (1975) charts the descent of a newly built tower block into anarchy as the residents, forced by the architecture into a kind of social stratification, turn in on themselves in a cycle of ever-increasing violence. Meanwhile, the building's architect, Anthony Royal, sits in his penthouse flat awaiting the final confrontation. Ballard's dystopia was not reality, of course, but the book's power stemmed from the way it took something plausible and extended it into the realm of fantasy. Indeed, the idea of an architect living at the top of one of his towers was clearly inspired by Ernő Goldfinger, who had lived with his wife in a flat near the top of his Balfron Tower in Poplar, east London, for three months shortly after its completion in 1968.

The demonisation of post-war architecture continued into the 1990s, even after the return to power of the Labour Party under Tony Blair in the guise of 'New Labour' in 1997. Amid the haze of 'Cool Britannia' – with the renewed popularity of 1960s' music and fashion linked to Brit Pop and football 'coming home' at Euro '96 three decades after England's 1966 World Cup success – architecture was conspicuously absent. A precise architectural contemporary of the Kinks' 1967 song 'Waterloo Sunset' was, after all, the Brutalist Southbank Centre.[18] The exclusion of architecture from the short-lived 1960s revival was an indication that, while the rhetoric and imagery were different, in economic terms New Labour was actually more of a continuation than a break from Thatcherite free-market policies. The market, not the state, remained the undisputed driving force of Britain's economy.

The Brutalist Southbank Centre (LCC, from 1967) sits on part of the old Festival of Britain site between the Royal Festival Hall and Waterloo Bridge.

Reassessment and revival

Although New Labour followed Thatcherism in its embrace of the market and the 'wealth-creators' of the banking and financial sectors, it differed by seeking to use taxation to pursue traditional social-democratic policies, investing in education and health. As Tony Blair's spin doctor Peter Mandelson put it in 1998, New Labour was 'intensely relaxed about people getting filthy rich', adding, in a phrase that is usually omitted, 'as long as they pay their taxes'.

His comment epitomised Blair's attempt to find a middle ground between untrammelled capitalism and socialism. This was the age of the 'public-private partnership' and of the 'private finance initiative' or PFI, in which the private sector put up the capital for and delivered major building projects, with the state repaying it over a number of years, thus keeping the expenditure off the government's balance sheet. But the private sector's involvement rarely stopped there, with many of the new facilities managed and run by privately owned public-service providers.[19]

Just as Modernism reflected the post-war era and Postmodernism the new economic freedoms of the 1980s, so the first decade of New Labour can be seen as having its own architectural language, one in which, thanks to PFI and an economic boom, public and private buildings are broadly indistinguishable. This was a language of intentionally irregular 'barcode façades', of cheap cladding and shiny surfaces, of bright colours and polished wood veneer, and of the mandatory lofty entrance hall or atrium leading to more generic spaces. Eschewing historicism or neo-vernacular, this was clearly a modern architecture, though a version shorn of the socially transformative mission of the post-war architecture it so frequently replaced. Freed of ideology, the buildings of New Labour were left simply to evoke the new.

It was this New Labour landscape that served as inspiration and subject for the critic Owen Hatherley's influential book, *A Guide to the New Ruins of Great Britain* (2010). The timing of the book's launch was pivotal, coming just after Labour's fall from power – a government visibly exhausted, out of ideas and discredited by the Iraq War. In his book, Hatherley combines a reappraisal of post-war British architecture, particularly Brutalism, with a series of sometimes vitriolic attacks on the architecture of the immediate past and of the economic system that he saw as having created it.

The considerable popular success that Hatherley has enjoyed with *New Ruins* and the books that followed is due at least in part to the way his work channelled so many of the frustrations and disappointments felt particularly by those on the left. More broadly, however, the book had powerful resonances within the context of the growing crisis of affordability in housing, with more and more people finding themselves unable to buy a place to live.

'Right to buy' had been maintained under New Labour and was promoted with renewed vigour by the Coalition and Conservative governments after 2010. As the supply of social

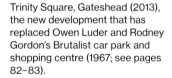

Trinity Square, Gateshead (2013), the new development that has replaced Owen Luder and Rodney Gordon's Brutalist car park and shopping centre (1967; see pages 82–83).

housing decreased, so more people were forced into the expensive and unstable private rental market. Many former council houses are now rented out by their owners privately, with in some instances the state paying out Housing Benefits to subsidise the rents being charged for properties it once owned.[20] At the same time, regeneration, particularly in London and south-east England, has seen large housing estates redeveloped privately, with the loss of hundreds of homes previously let at social rents.

By placing into sharp relief the contrasts between the laissez-faire attitudes of the present and the interventionist policies of the post-war era, Hatherley generated a degree of nostalgia, especially among those on the left who looked longingly towards the fairer, more equitable (if rather poorer) country that existed before Thatcher. But for those who had lived through the era – even those like the critic Jonathan Meades who are sympathetic to Brutalism – the idea that it represents some kind of golden age is received with incredulity.[21] Enthusiasm for that moment is one thing, yet Hatherley's account is clearly selective in a way that suits his political purposes. As the architectural historian Mark Crinson has recently noted,[22] it is telling that Hatherley focuses on the Park Hill estate in Sheffield and not, say, Robin Hood Gardens in London: the first was designed by local-authority architects and therefore fits his narrative, while the second, by the private practice of Alison and Peter Smithson, does so rather less neatly.

Concrete futures

The popularity that Brutalism in particular, and post-war architecture more broadly, currently enjoys is an extraordinary reversal from even a decade ago. Brutalism's fashionability has risen, not just through traditional media like books or journalism, but notably online. The last few years have seen proliferating social-media accounts tweeting and instagramming photographs of concrete buildings to growing audiences of aficionados.[23] In an online world where what we share on social media becomes part of our idealised self-image, retweeting a photo of a post-war housing block is a way of aligning oneself with a kind of counter-cultural trendiness that plays on post-war architecture's former pariah status, while also implying a vague and suitably non-committal alignment with leftist politics. In this sphere, Brutalism in particular has become a shareable – and tradeable – currency of cool.

While the revival of interest in post-war architecture could only have happened in the way it has at this particular moment, there is a broader issue of the cyclical nature of

Park Hill, Sheffield (Jack Lynn and Ivor Smith for Sheffield Corporation, 1961), which has been extensively refurbished by Hawkins\Brown and Studio Egret for developer Urban Splash.

taste. It is often noted how generations actively turn against the tastes of their parents' generation, but sometimes quite like that of their grandparents. First-generation Modernists of the 1920s and 1930s, for example, reviled Victorian architecture but admired that of the Georgians – and so it has continued to the present. It is no coincidence that it is among those born in the 1980s or later that admiration for Brutalism has taken root. There is, furthermore, a certain frisson in embracing the unfashionable or even the despised, one that was enjoyed by early advocates for a reappraisal of Brutalism in the 1990s and 2000s as much as by those who had pioneered the reassessment of Victorian architecture in the 1950s.[24]

As post-war architecture has returned to fashionability, its value has increased, both culturally and economically. A few years ago one had to go back at least to the nineteenth century before a house became a 'period property'; now a post-war council flat (at least if it is one of the more architecturally interesting examples) can be considered in a similar way. The rise of estate agents like The Modern House, which specialises in selling both pre- and post-war properties with designer cachet, reveals just how sought-after the architecture of these eras is becoming. This is also reflected in the current redevelopment of council-built Balfron Tower in east London and the former office building Centre Point in central London as private flats. The National Trust runs tours of Brutalist buildings and even opened a pop-up flat in Balfron to the public in 2014. So accepted has Brutalism become that some of its most famous landmarks now appear on T-shirts, mugs and tea towels. Concrete, it seems, has become 'heritage' – that strange, politically inert and consumer-ready category, in which the past is frozen and its connections to our present moment are severed. That Brutalism, the most confrontational of post-war styles, has been sanitised in this way is surely evidence of how its buildings and the values they embody are no longer deemed to pose any kind of challenge to the status quo.

While some have lamented the depoliticisation of post-war architecture, the important trade-off is that renewed interest in its aesthetics has played a key role in securing a future for buildings that were until recently at risk. Losses will inevitably continue, but as a growing number of the best buildings of the era are protected by listing, the status of post-war architecture can only grow, with more and more people casting off prejudice and beginning to experience and understand for themselves. If heritage deals ultimately with an image of the past, the materiality of a building exists in a quite different realm. When faced by a building like the recently listed Preston Bus Station, for example, it is impossible not to feel its boldness, overwhelming scale and unflinching nature as somehow transcending time and place. Its builders did not shy away from the future, but actively tried to shape it; the building stands as that ambition to change the world made concrete.

Experiencing such buildings for oneself reveals them to be so much more than simply the embodiment of the welfare state, as some would have us believe. Moreover, to explore the thinking behind post-war architecture's most polemical strand – Brutalism – is to discover both its origins in the experience of the Victorian city and the ruins of war, and its profound interest in the advent of consumerist societies. Architecture was, in fact, just one manifestation of a much broader artistic movement that encompassed the experimental photographs of Nigel Henderson, the mechanistic sculptures of Eduardo Paolozzi and the Pop Art collages of Richard Hamilton.[25] Although the view of Brutalism as a purely architectural movement appeals to leftist writers like Hatherley, for whom it stands as Modernism at its most militant, in reality it was a strange and ambiguous cultural phenomenon. And while it dominates debates, both then and now, Brutalism is, of course, just one constituent of a much wider landscape of post-war architecture.

Preston Bus Station (Building Design Partnership, 1969), which has recently been listed after a succession of attempts at demolition.

A more nuanced, more complex and ultimately heterogeneous view of post-war architecture, which can be gained only from experience of the buildings themselves, is valuable not just for its own sake but also for what it can offer in helping us to address the social, economic and political upheavals of our own time. Just as the consensus that emerged after the war ended in the 1970s, so the one that has dominated since the early 1980s is drawing to a close. The need for alternatives is clear. This is not, however, to suggest a return to the policies of the post-war era, for example, in advocating a new generation of council housing. The ideas that were put into practice then emerged in response to a very particular set of conditions; those we have now are fundamentally different. As we look towards the most significant challenges we face over the next few decades – climate change, mass migration, the further decline of the influence of the nation state, the social and economic consequences of automation – it is clear that new ideas, new ways of doing things and new ways of pooling our resources need to be found. Faced with the establishment mantra of 'there is no alternative', the architecture of the post-war era provides physical evidence that the system and values we have today are not those we have always had – and despite appearances, these can be changed, even dramatically.

The following pages feature 35 buildings put up in Britain during the post-war era (defined as 1945–79), which have been demolished or heavily altered – or are imminently facing either of those fates. They range across different types – from schools and libraries to factories and power stations – and locations. Inevitably, because of the volume both built and demolished, housing comprises a significant proportion of the buildings included. At the same time, the pace of redevelopment in south-east England means that there are more buildings included from this area than any other. Needless to say, it is impossible to be comprehensive; several notable losses are not included, as well as thousands of other buildings that have simply gone, leaving no trace other than in the memories of those who lived or worked in them.

Running in parallel to the critical reappraisal of post-war architecture, recent years have seen a range of projects exploring the capacity of buildings, particularly housing, to act as records or even memorials through the physical traces of patterns of everyday life etched into their spaces.[26] This book, however, takes a rather different approach, by representing all the buildings in their original state through photographs taken in the year of their completion or shortly afterwards. In doing so, it intentionally avoids invoking the ways post-war architecture can become a repository for memory, and instead focuses on the contrast between the buildings' intended futures and their ultimate fates.

Almost all of the photographs in this book were taken by photographers working for the Architectural Press, the archive of which is now held by the RIBA in London. Although working to a clear brief in photographing buildings for publication, the photographers each brought their own particular sensibilities to the task. Some, such as John Donat, brought a deep interest in the everyday realities of the ways the buildings would be used and by whom (see, for instance, pages 77 and 92–93); others, like Henk Snoek, looked to the drama of the composition, aiming to convey in their images how transformative these buildings aspired to be (pages 43, 44–45). But despite these differences in approach, as a group the photographs are consistent in conjuring a sense of optimism, of the world changing for the better, showing the intentions of architect, client and builder in their best light, however flawed they turned out to be. Seeing this towering ambition laid bare, the photographs in this book offer us a haunting glimpse of a future that never quite happened.

Buildings

Freemasons Estate

Newham, London
1965–72

Demolished in
1986

Architect,
London Borough
of Newham

Unknown
photographer,
1984

During the 1960s prefabrication and 'system build' became increasingly prevalent in housing construction. Manufacturing building components off-site allowed housing to be delivered more cheaply and more quickly than traditional methods, while also mitigating the effects of skills shortages in the building trade. But as politicians, both Labour and Conservative, played a continual game of one-upmanship over who could promise and deliver more housing, quality frequently suffered. Leaks, damp and infestations became common problems.

One of the most important prefabrication systems was that produced by the Danish company, Larsen & Nielsen, which specialised in concrete panels that included windows, doors and all necessary ducts – and sold in the volumes needed to make factory fabrication economically viable. The Larsen & Nielsen system was used in a building of more than twenty storeys for the first time in a development of eight towers at the Freemasons Estate in Canning Town, begun in 1965 by Taylor Woodrow Anglian for the London Borough of Newham.

Only two months after people had moved into one of these towers – Ronan Point (the one furthest in the distance in the photograph) – a gas explosion on the eighteenth floor caused the whole corner of the building to collapse, killing four people and injuring many others. An inquiry revealed that the joints between panels had been too weak, and thus the structure was unable to withstand even a small explosion; the person who had lit the ill-fated match that ignited the gas had survived with just minor injuries.

Subsequent legislation ensured that such a tragedy would be impossible in the future, but public confidence in system-built towers was irreparably damaged. Ronan Point itself was repaired with reinforced joints and stood for another eighteen years until its demolition in 1986.

The Dover Stage Hotel

Dover, Kent, 1957

Demolished in 1988

Architect, Louis Erdi

Photographed by Reginald Hugo de Burgh Galwey in 1957

The Dover Stage Hotel was one of the first hotels to be built in Britain after the Second World War. It stood on the seafront site of an early nineteenth-century building called the Round House, which had been occupied by the British Legion and, briefly, by a gospel mission, before its near-total destruction by enemy action during the war. The lease for the site was acquired by the brewers, Watney, Combe & Reid in the late 1940s and it was they who eventually erected the hotel in 1957.

The design by Louis Erdi was described by the *Kent Messenger* in an article reporting on the beginning of building work as 'ultramodern' – and in many ways it was. It comprised five floors of bedrooms elevated two storeys into the air on spindly V-shaped pilotis. The rectilinear concrete frame was left exposed, with the structure extending seamlessly into the service unit that poked above the horizontal roof line. Each of the bedrooms had its own balcony, angled to get the best sea views and sunlight. Underneath the bedroom block ran a low range containing bars, restaurant facilities and a ballroom.

The hotel was intended to cater for the coach trade arriving by ferry from the continent. It was initially successful, but as visitors' requirements and expectations rose over the following decades the rooms appeared increasingly small. The hotel changed hands several times during the 1970s and 1980s before closing and being demolished in 1988, ostensibly to make way for a new hotel. However, the plans fell through and the plum site next to the elegant Regency Camden Crescent, overlooking Granville Gardens with the sea beyond, became a car park, which it remains to this day.

Serpentine Restaurant

Hyde Park, London, 1964   Demolished in 1990   Architect, Patrick Gwynne   Photographed by John Donat in 1964

Patrick Gwynne was best known for his private house commissions, but he also developed a reputation as a designer of restaurants, with the Serpentine Restaurant in London's Hyde Park one of his finest. After a pupilage with Ernest Coleridge, who was himself trained by Edwin Lutyens, Gwynne found work with Wells Coates, one of the founders of the Modern Architectural Research Group (MARS). In contrast to the traditionalism of Coleridge, Gwynne was now immersed in Modernism, which he put into practice, while working in Coates's office, by designing a house for his parents in Surrey. This became The Homewood, the building for which Gwynne is best known, a boldly assured architectural statement inspired by two seminal works of pre-war Modernism: Le Corbusier's Villa Savoye near Paris and Mies van der Rohe's Villa Tugendhat in Brno. Gywnne's parents only lived in the house for a short while; in 1946 he moved in himself and made various changes to suit his needs. The house is now owned by the National Trust.

After the war, which he spent in the Royal Air Force helping to build airfields, Gwynne entered and narrowly lost the competition for the restaurant for the Festival of Britain. Despite the disappointment, he soon gained the commission for the Crescent Restaurant at Battersea Funfair. This success won him the attention of the Forte restaurant group and the task of designing two new restaurants in Hyde Park.

Overlooking Hyde Park's famous lake, the Serpentine Restaurant was an arresting structure, comprising a series of concrete 'mushrooms' which sprouted from thin points in the ground to form wide canopies above. Adjoining heavier concrete forms provided a platform from which rose a series of glazed umbrella-like structures. The whole scheme was carefully composed to hide service elements, including the car park, while providing great views of the lake and informal shelter when necessary. The Serpentine Restaurant was demolished in 1990, but the contemporary Dell Restaurant nearby, also by Gwynne, still survives and is now listed.

Southgate Estate

Runcorn New Town, Cheshire, 1977

Demolished between 1990 and 1992

Architect, James Stirling

Photographed by Roy Herman Kantorowich in 1968

When James Stirling's Southgate Estate in Runcorn New Town was demolished in 1992, just fifteen years after its completion, the *Architects' Journal* described it as 'Britain's Pruitt-Igoe' – invoking the large housing project outside St Louis, Missouri, designed in the mid-1950s by Minoru Yamasaki. The beginning of Pruitt-Igoe's destruction in 1972 was declared by the critic Charles Jencks to signal the death of Modernism. By the early 1990s, popular opinion had long since turned against such large-scale estates with deck access, raw concrete and uncompromisingly Modernist design. So when the Warrington and Runcorn Development Corporation, which had commissioned Southgate, sought to clear itself of significant liabilities before being wound up in 1989, few protested at the loss of an estate that in almost everyone's eyes had decisively failed.

In reality, as in other housing complexes of the era, many of the problems at Southgate had relatively little to do with decisions made by the architect and much more to do with those imposed by the client: the low budget, which meant a cheap and quick industrial construction system with heavy prefabricated concrete slabs had to be used; lack of insulation; oil-based communal heating that many residents were unable to afford; and a high turnover of tenants, creating a social mix ill-suited to the elevated deck access.

That said, few residents ever warmed to Stirling's abstraction of the façades and squares of Georgian Bath and attempts at enlivening the system-built construction. In photographs, its heavy concrete geometries, garishly coloured glass-reinforced plastic (GRP) panels and exposed pipework give it an oddly placeless feel, more like something from a 1970s sci-fi film than a realistic proposition as a place where people might live. Ultimately, the architecture was simply unable to overcome the harsh constraints of an industrial construction system.

Reliance Controls Factory

Swindon, Wiltshire, 1967

Demolished in 1991

Architect, Team 4

Photographed by Bill Toomey in 1967

Richard Rogers and Norman Foster met while both were studying at Yale in the early 1960s. On their return to the UK, they founded Team 4 with Su Brumwell and Wendy Cheesman in 1963, going on to design several important houses before a split in 1967 and the beginning of their own respective practices. Team 4's house designs were closely inspired by what the architects had seen in the US, notably works by Frank Lloyd Wright and Louis Kahn, as well as the California Case Study Houses, particularly that by Charles and Ray Eames. All of these sources, as well as Alison and Peter Smithson's steel-framed Hunstanton School, proved important influences when the young practice was commissioned by the Reliance Controls electronics company to design a factory in Swindon.

The demanding brief was for a factory that would be cheap and buildable in just ten months. Moreover, this was to be a new type of factory building that reflected the dawning age of electronics and broke down the traditional hierarchical distinctions between workers and management. Team 4's response was a prefabricated steel-frame structure enclosing a single space of more than 3000 square metres, which allowed the interior arrangement to be changed very easily. Outside, the steel members were painted white to provide a visual contrast to the grey corrugated-steel cladding. In all areas of the design clever solutions were found to save both time and money: for example, the fluorescent striplights were inserted into the grooves of the corrugated cladding, removing the need for both plastic surrounds and reflectors.

In its clear expression of the building's structure and the flexibility afforded by the steel frame, Reliance Controls was an early example of what became known as 'High-Tech', a movement in which Rogers and Foster were key players. Team 4 broke up before the building's completion, and, despite its obvious importance in the subsequent course of late twentieth-century British architecture, it was demolished in 1991.

Queen Elizabeth Square

Hutchesontown C, Gorbals, Glasgow, 1965

Demolished in 1993

Architect, Sir Basil Spence

Photographed by Henk Snoek in 1967

In 1945, Glasgow Corporation published the 'Bruce Report', named after its author, Robert Bruce, the city's chief engineer. Charged with devising proposals to alleviate the decay and poverty afflicting much of the city's housing stock, Bruce made recommendations that could not have been more radical, advocating the wholesale destruction of much of the city centre, including architectural gems such as Glasgow Central Station and Charles Rennie Mackintosh's Glasgow School of Art. In its place, Bruce imagined a clean, modern and rationally planned city comprising multiple series of tower blocks and a motorway ring road.

Bruce's proposals proved too extreme even for Glasgow's ambitious councillors and the plan was never enacted. Several of its proposals did, however, provide the basis for subsequent regeneration initiatives, notably the driving of what is now the M8 motorway through the heart of the city, the destruction of vast swathes of slum dwellings, and the creation of new estates outside the city centre. Of these, Basil Spence's Hutchesontown C in the Gorbals

was among the most notorious – and ultimately short-lived.

The Gorbals was one of the city's poorest areas and an obvious candidate for comprehensive redevelopment. A multi-stage plan was produced with Spence responsible for 400 dwellings. These were organised in two modular slabs, essentially ten towers standing on dramatically splayed pilotis, connected by adjacent balconies. With the lifts only stopping at every other floor to save money, dwellings alternated between flats and maisonettes.

Despite achieving many of the project's aims, such as maintaining the high density of the area and incorporating easy access to green space both between and within the blocks (via the large balconies), the flats quickly deteriorated, succumbing to damp and infestation. By the 1990s, Hutchesontown C was widely perceived as a failure, and with the council facing a multimillion pound renovation bill, it was decided to demolish, despite the vehement protests of some, including the campaigners for Modernist architecture, Docomomo-UK.

Hulme Crescents

Manchester, 1972

Demolished in 1994

Architect, Hugh Wilson and J. Lewis Womersley

Unknown photographer

When completed in 1972, Hulme Crescents, which covered a huge area to the south of Manchester city centre, was one of the largest city-regeneration projects in Europe. The estate comprised four vast crescent-shaped blocks named after major figures in British architectural history: John Nash, William Kent, Charles Barry and Robert Adam. The naming was, however, more than a piece of optimistic whimsy. The architects, Hugh Wilson and J. Lewis Womersley, best known for their work as chief architects at Cumbernauld and Sheffield respectively, had chosen the shape to evoke the great Georgian crescents of Bath and London. At Hulme, the crescents were constructed with prefabricated concrete panels, deck access and elevated walkways linking adjacent ranges. Even before the Ronan Point disaster of 1968, public opinion had begun to turn against tower blocks, so Hulme Crescents was always conceived to be low-rise.

The estate was beset by problems from the very beginning, thanks to a combination of design faults and poor construction.

Leaks were widespread, while the underfloor heating system proved too expensive for many tenants to run. Infestation was also a major issue, with the long ducts that linked the communal heating system proving attractive to mice and cockroaches. Within two years of the estate's completion, it was deemed unfit for families.

By 1984, the council stopped collecting rents and virtually abandoned the estate, prompting the arrival of Manchester's burgeoning art, music and party scene. While Tony Wilson's Haçienda is remembered as the defining nightclub of the era, The Kitchen, which occupied three Hulme Crescents flats knocked together, was for many the true heart of the 'Madchester' music world. Everyone from MCs and graffiti artists to drug dealers and prostitutes flocked to the estate, finding inspiration and freedom in its abandoned spaces.

The party could not go on forever, however, and in 1991 the council was allocated money by central government to revive its housing stock. Hulme Crescents was demolished three years later.

Stifford Estate with 'Old Flo'

Stepney, London, 1961 (sculpture installed 1962)

Estate demolished in 1999, with 'Old Flo' loaned to Yorkshire Sculpture Park in 1997

Architect, LCC Architects' Department; sculpture by Henry Moore

Unknown photographer

Henry Moore's sculpture *Draped Seated Woman* (1957–58), popularly known as 'Old Flo', is all that remains of the Stifford Estate in Stepney, east London, which was demolished in 1999. The sculpture is currently installed at the Yorkshire Sculpture Park, to whom it was loaned, essentially for safekeeping, by Tower Hamlets Council. It made headlines in 2012 when Tower Hamlets attempted to sell it, prompting a legal battle over ownership that was only resolved in the High Court in 2015.

The sculpture was originally acquired for £7,000 by the LCC in 1961 using funds from its Patronage of the Arts Scheme, which allocated 0.1% of its buildings budget for the purchase of artworks. The background to this initiative was the considerable popular success the LCC had achieved with a series of modern sculpture exhibitions held in Battersea Park from 1948, which had furthered the idea that public art could help create a sense of community and identity in new schools and housing estates.

However, the purchase or commissioning of public art was far from straightforward. One of the principal difficulties was balancing the need for work with which local people could identify with artistic quality and credibility that might stand the test of time. Moreover, there was a tension between purchasing pre-existing pieces by well-known artists like Moore and commissioning artists to produce work that was site-specific, often in close collaboration with the architects. In the end, the Stifford Estate contained examples of both, with the artist Anthony Holloway creating a series of murals for the point blocks using cheap everyday materials such as tile, mosaic and concrete.

Holloway's work at the Stifford Estate was lost when its tower blocks were demolished. However, similar work by him survives at the later Brandon Estate in Kennington, south London, for which, coincidentally, another work by Moore (*Reclining Figure No. 3*) was bought and remains in situ.

Gleadless Valley Estate

Sheffield, 1962

One of the three towers has been demolished, with the remaining two re-clad in 1998

Architect, Sheffield Corporation City Architect's Department

Photographed by Telegraph & Star Studios in 1963

The Gleadless Valley Estate lies on one of the hills to the south of Sheffield city centre, surrounding a wooded valley called Meers Brook. The site was considered for housing in the 1930s but deemed too steep; however, by the 1950s, with land at a comparative premium, such difficulties became less important. The project was overseen by J. Lewis Womersley, head of Sheffield's city architect's department, then one of the most attractive destinations for young forward-thinking architects.

As a consequence of the site's undulating topography, it contains a mixture of building types. Among the most striking are the six-storey blocks of maisonettes, which are reached by bridges from the nearby road; they meet the blocks half way up, making lifts unnecessary. The architects could not have been unaware of the medieval feel of what they designed.

The three towers shown in this photograph looking down Constable Road were notable local landmarks and visible from the city centre.

Only two remain. The third was demolished in 1995, apparently because of unstable foundations, and the others were reclad at around the same time. In 2008, with the estate mired in crime and myriad social problems, Sheffield's *Star* newspaper ran a story asking whether Gleadless Valley was the worst estate in the city. As ever, the description was more to do with lack of employment opportunities than the architecture, which is generally well regarded.

Although unremarkable architecturally, Gleadless Valley is now comparatively well known as the setting for the film *This is England* (2006) and the TV series of the same name, both written and directed by Shane Meadows. The film is set in the early 1980s and follows the chaotic lives of a group of skinheads in the council estates of a fictional Midlands coastal town. Much of the TV series was shot at Gleadless Valley, which is depicted apparently very little changed from the time it was built.

Hinkley Point A nuclear power station

Near Bridgwater, Somerset, 1964

Decommissioned in 2000; demolition ongoing

Architect, Sir Frederick Gibberd

Photographed by Henk Snoek in 1964

While still dependent on coal as its principal source of energy, during the 1950s Britain was arguably the world leader in harnessing the power of the atom for civilian electricity production. The first nuclear reactor to operate commercially anywhere in the world was opened at Windscale, Cumbria, in 1956 and, despite a serious fire at the site the following year, the government embarked on a huge nuclear power station building programme. A slew of power stations opened over the next decade, based on Magnox reactor technology, which was originally developed to produce plutonium for nuclear weapons.

Hinkley Point A on the north Somerset coast opened in 1965, built by a consortium of English Electric, Babcock & Wilcox and Taylor Woodrow, with Frederick Gibberd as consultant architect. The station rose above the coastline in a functional yet highly monumental composition of two box-like reactor halls and a long, lower-rise block. Although built for civilian use, Hinkley Point's reactors included a modification ensuring that, if the need arose, they could produce weapons-grade plutonium.

By the 1990s the early Magnox-based power stations were reaching the end of their lives. In 2000, faced with numerous maintenance issues, it was decided to close Hinkley Point A, while the later B station would continue to produce electricity for a further decade. Over the course of its 35 years in operation, Hinkley Point A produced 103 TWh of electricity, said to be enough to supply the whole of the UK for a year. The power station is being gradually demolished, while arguments about the procurement and funding of a potential successor – Hinkley Point C – continue.

Brynmawr Rubber Factory

Brynmawr, Gwent, 1951

Demolished in 2001

Architect, Architects' Co-Partnership

Photographed by Reginald Hugo de Burgh Galwey in 1952

The Brynmawr Rubber Factory was one of the great architectural follies of the post-war era: built to fulfil a need that did not yet exist, overly ambitious architecturally and ultimately doomed to failure. Despite all that, however, the building was a major and influential architectural achievement on the part of its young designers, Peter Cocke and Michael Powers, and their practice, the Architects' Co-Partnership, together with the building's engineers, Ove Arup and his partner Ronald Jenkins.

The idea for the factory had emerged as a response to the unemployment brought about by the downturn in the fortunes of the South Wales coalfields before the war. A socialist peer, Jim Forrester, saw an opportunity to alleviate the area's social and economic ills by establishing a new factory there for his Brimstone Rubber Company. Having managed to convince the government to invest in the scheme, Forrester went to Cocke and Powers for a design that would embody his bold democratic ambitions for the factory: a single entrance and canteen for both workers and management, and on-site health and welfare facilities for staff.

With building materials still in relatively short supply, the engineers proposed the idea of a concrete-shell structure. The result was nine shallow domes supported only by their pedentives, allowing the creation of vast interior open spaces, lit by wide windows at the dome edge and perimeter walls. The overall effect, particularly at night, was almost Byzantine in its economy of expression and spatial clarity.

Unfortunately, Forrester's ambitious plans for the factory failed and he was forced to sell to Dunlop Semtex, which redeployed the building for manufacturing rubber floors. It continued operating until 1982, but never at the capacity originally envisaged, and quickly fell into disrepair after its closure. Despite attempts to find alternative uses and restore the building – and the fact that it was the first post-war building in Wales to be listed – the factory was demolished in 2001.

Alexander Fleming House

Southwark, London Blocks A–C, 1959–63; blocks D, E and Odeon cinema, 1964–67

Cinema demolished in 1988; the remainder converted into flats in 2002

Architect, Ernő Goldfinger

Photographed by Reginald Hugo de Burgh Galwey in 1966

When the first part of Alexander Fleming House, on the Elephant and Castle roundabout in central south London, was completed in 1963 it was met with near-universal acclaim. Widely praised in the press, it won awards and was regarded by its architect, the Hungarian émigré Ernő Goldfinger, as one of his best works. However, by the 1990s its star had long since fallen; it narrowly escaped the wrecking ball, and survives now only in considerably altered form.

The site on the corner between Newington Causeway and New Kent Road had been earmarked for redevelopment by the LCC in 1956. The initial intention had been to retain the huge, 3500-seat Trocadero cinema, with its famous Wurlitzer organ. However, once the site was sold, it was decided instead to demolish the theatre and undertake a more comprehensive redevelopment. Goldfinger was brought in and he devised a configuration of three blocks arranged around an open piazza and pond. At this stage the building's use was still to be determined, so Goldfinger designed in a great degree of flexibility.

On completion, the three blocks were occupied by the Department of Health, which named the building Alexander Fleming House after the discoverer of penicillin. Two further blocks and the Odeon cinema, all to Goldfinger's design, were added between 1964 and 1967. Problems soon emerged, however, with the ventilation and glazing systems, and also with traffic noise, all partly as a result of how cheaply the building had been constructed.

In 1989, the Department of Health left and the building remained empty until its conversion into flats in 2002 (the cinema was demolished in 1988). As well as a substantial reordering of the interior, the conversion saw significant alterations to the exterior: the painting of the original raw concrete; the covering of the window spandrel panels in a sky-blue film; and the enclosing of the originally publicly accessible space around which the blocks were composed. Although these changes are largely detrimental to the building as conceived, the essence of Goldfinger's complex fusing of Russian Constructivist compositional principles with a classically inspired post-and-beam system remains more or less intact and helped ensure the building's listing in 2013.

Dacorum Pavilion

Hemel
Hempstead,
1966

Closed in 2002
and demolished
soon after

Architect,
Clifford Culpin
& Partners

Photographed
by Henk Snoek
in 1966

Hemel Hempstead was one of the first wave of new towns founded under the New Towns Act of 1946. In spirit and in form they were heavily influenced by the ideas of the Garden City movement and its early manifestations, notably at Welwyn. The movement had emerged in the late nineteenth century, pioneered in the writings of Ebenezer Howard, who held that the industrial city was no longer tenable as a place for people to live. In contrast to the squalor and overcrowding of urban environments, he proposed a new type of conurbation, half town and half country, rationally planned and built at a low density with large amounts of green space, and largely self-sufficient, with agriculture and industry nearby.

The Garden City was therefore the obvious model for the new towns that aimed to attract people out of central London. Hemel Hempstead was something of an exception, however, in that it was already a settlement of more than 21,000 people, with a history that went as far back as William the Conqueror's Domesday Book.

The original plan for the town, drawn up by Geoffrey Jellicoe, retained parts of the 'old town', with a new town centre built to the south along Marlowes, which runs parallel with the River Gade. Around this, he proposed a series of satellite housing developments, each with its own distinct identity.

Jellicoe's initial scheme for the town centre proved too ambitious, and a revised version was eventually approved in 1952. The Dacorum Pavilion arrived in the mid-1960s – a plain but elegant community performance venue designed by Clifford Culpin who, with his father Ewart, had produced strikingly modern town halls for Greenwich and Poplar before the war.

Over the years, the Pavilion played host to major acts including U2, David Bowie and Eric Clapton. It closed in 2002 on the pretext that a modern venue would replace it on the same site. However, more than a decade later no new building has emerged and local people continue to lament the loss of an important community asset.

Harlow was one of the first new towns built after the Second World War. Unlike Hemel Hempstead, for example, which was already a reasonably sized conurbation, there was little community to speak of at Harlow's designated site, so development was able to proceed on green fields with little resistance. Of all the new towns, Harlow is more the product of a single overarching vision than any other: that of Frederick Gibberd.

Gibberd's scheme was based on an axial road running south from the railway station to a small hill where he placed the town centre, called the High. He felt strongly that landscape was essential to give new places meaning, so he arranged the plan around the existing streams and valleys, which he left open as pockets of green running through the development. While Gibberd's team was responsible for much of the housing built, he also engaged other architects who worked in a private capacity, including such notable figures as Maxwell Fry, Philip Powell, Jacko Moya, F.R.S. Yorke and H.T. Cadbury-Brown.

Gibberd was a firm believer in the value of public sculpture, and as a consequence Harlow is renowned for its extensive collection, which includes work by a number of significant artists.

The greatest set-piece, where art, architecture and landscape came together, was the Water Gardens. Unfolding in front of the civic centre – a tower intended to be visible from all over the town – Gibberd created three terraces stepping down the slope; two large ponds occupied the two top terraces, with the bottom one containing seven different pools. Sculpted lion heads by William Mitchell ornamented the retaining walls, with other sculptures, such as the one by Karel Vogel to the left in this photograph, laid around the gardens. The overall impression through the changes of scale and planting was of the rigid plan giving way to an informality that connected the gardens to the surrounding landscape.

Gibberd's landmark tower was demolished in 2003 in a major redevelopment of the town centre. The Water Gardens survive in a new location, having given their name to the large shopping centre that now surrounds them.

Tricorn Shopping Centre

Portsmouth, Hampshire, 1965

Demolished in 2004

Architect, Owen Luder Partnership

Photographed by Sam Lambert in 1965

It is relatively unusual for an architect to be able to draw together the thinking behind a project in a few succinct sentences. But that is precisely what Owen Luder managed when defending his Tricorn Centre in Portsmouth after it had been included in 1967 in a *Daily Mail* poll of Britain's ugliest buildings:

> *We deliberately set out to get a Casbah feeling into the market and to make it aggressive. After all, shopping is an aggressive thing. Portsmouth is a pretty nondescript city, and at least we have now built something which will make people stop and stare. It is not streamlined or slick because it is not intended to be. If you have done your job properly, you will be ten years ahead and the public will not have caught up.*

Anyone who saw the Tricorn Centre, which was demolished in 2004, will attest to the sincerity of Luder's vision. Few buildings were quite as bloody-minded in their attitude to their surroundings and their users. For many observers, the Tricorn Centre put the 'brutal' into Brutalism; yet for others, it was one of that movement's greatest monuments, a building with strikingly sculptural energy.

As with Luder's other major key work of the early 1960s, Trinity Square in Gateshead, the Tricorn Centre combined a market with retail units and car park, as well as pubs, a restaurant, a nightclub and originally several flats. The placement of the market on the first storey and the need for it to be accessible to large lorries ensured a certain massiveness in the structure, while the low budget dictated the roughness of the finishes. The response of Luder and his collaborator Rodney Gordon was simply to emphasise these qualities with complex geometries, bold spans and spiralling access ramps.

The result was so overpowering that it seems unlikely the Tricorn Centre would have succeeded commercially even if its key shop units had been large enough to attract major retailers and its walkways better connected to the surroundings. Nevertheless, attempts were made to get it listed during the 1990s. Its eventual loss after decades of neglect and decay was lamented by many observers – though celebrated by rather more.

Mondial House, International Telephone Exchange

Upper Thames Street, London, 1975

Demolished in 2005

Architect, Hubbard Ford & Partners

Photographed by Martin Charles in 1975

The streams of commuters making their daily pilgrimage from London Bridge Station across the Thames to the City of London could scarcely have failed to notice the strange, futuristic building looming on the north bank of the river. Until the arrival of Terry Farrell's Postmodern twins of the MI6 (or SIS) Building at Vauxhall Cross and Embankment Place above Charing Cross Station, Mondial House was without doubt the most striking twentieth-century building to address London's great natural artery directly.

Mondial House's unusual appearance was at least in part a consequence of its unusual function: an international telephone exchange. It was a 'working building', designed primarily to house not people but a complex system of switches, cables and terminals, as well as the means to power and ventilate them (though there was also some accommodation for staff). The building's concrete structure was clad in distinctive white reinforced plastic – which always retained its brilliance – with thin strips of almost black windows. This arrangement, coupled with the odd protrusions rising on its river side, gave the exchange an abstract, scaleless quality, provoking Prince Charles to remark how to his eyes it resembled a 'word processor'. To others, though, it was a stark but wonderfully idiosyncratic statement of 1970s modernity.

Much of what Mondial House was designed to contain soon became out of date and digital technology needed far less space. As a result, Mondial House's days were always going to be numbered. BT closed and then sold it at auction in 2004, after which it was demolished and replaced by an office building.

Birmingham Post & Mail Building

Colmore Circus, Birmingham, 1965

Demolished in 2005

Architect, John H. D. Madin & Partners

Unknown photographer, 1968

Until its demolition in 2005, the Birmingham Post & Mail Building was one of the city's sleekest towers. Its seventeen storeys of glass, anodised aluminium, Argentinian granite and Sicilian marble, arranged in a neat rectilinear grid, appeared as a mini version of the ultra-refined, Miesian International Modernism more typically found in Midtown Manhattan. The tower, which contained offices for the *Birmingham Post* and *Evening Mail* newspapers, an advertisement hall and even a flat for the newspapers' director, was raised up on a large podium, a configuration inspired by Skidmore, Owings & Merrill's Lever House in New York (1951–52). In Birmingham, the podium contained the newspapers' heavy printing presses, and as a result the tight grid of the tower gave way to a wider, more robust arrangement of steel piers that reflected the industrial activities taking place within it. Most of the podium was actually left unglazed, with windows inserted only where production offices lay behind.

For the building's architects, John H. D. Madin & Partners (D. V. Smith was the partner in charge, working with project architects Ronald E. Cordin and Ramon K. Wood), the Birmingham Post & Mail Building was one of their greatest achievements, rivalled only by their Birmingham Central Library, completed ten years later. At first glance, these two buildings could not be more different in both formal arrangement and materials – neatly encapsulating how during this period, particularly in the USA but also in Britain, concrete was typically used for public buildings while steel and glass were reserved for commercial applications. However, both buildings were united by their attention to surface detailing – and each in its own way stood as a powerful symbol of a city reborn after the devastation of the Second World War.

Southside Halls of Residence

Imperial College, Kensington, London, 1963

Demolished in 2005

Architect, Richard Sheppard, Robson & Partners

Photographed by John Donat in 1963

Southside Halls of Residence at Imperial College in London was one of Britain's first university buildings to be directly inspired by the work of Le Corbusier, notably his Unité d'habitation apartments in Marseille (1947–52). Like Corb's seminal block, Southside comprised a slab with a rectilinear concrete frame, with an elevated walkway inspired by the Unité's internal streets and not dissimilar to the 'streets in the sky' that had begun to feature in contemporary housing. As well as student rooms, Southside contained cafeterias, communal areas and a famous bar, looking out on to the gentle greenery of Kensington's Prince's Gardens. Like the best university residences, Southside managed to combine an air of sobriety, befitting a place of serious study, with a sense that university is also a place for enjoyment, exemplified in the sculptural flourishes of the spiral stairs and the joy taken in the concrete detailing.

Southside was preceded by the smaller Weeks Hall (completed in 1957) on the opposite side of Prince's Gardens, which was intended in part as a prototype for the larger development. When construction began on Southside, considerable savings were made in the building's structure in comparison with the earlier building. The reinforcement bars of its prefabricated panels were covered by just 10 mm of concrete. As a result, repairs began just four years after completion. By the time it was scheduled for demolition in the mid-2000s, the walkway was netted off after large chunks of concrete had fallen from the structure, while the building was constantly plagued by temperature fluctuations that proved impossible to solve. Moreover, because the building had been designed so specifically for its purpose, it proved very difficult to adapt it to meet modern standards and conditions: internal walls were often fixed, while services were hidden deep inside the concrete structure.

Although Southside was listed Grade II, given the various and fundamental problems with the building, even its supporters had to concede that renovation was not a realistic option. Demolition began in 2005, but on the condition that Weeks Hall was retained and refurbished. Southside was replaced by a modern hall of residence designed by Kohn Pedersen Fox as part of a broader masterplan for the area.

Bargates
Shopping Centre

Burton-on-Trent, Staffordshire, 1967

Closed in 2007 and demolished in 2012

Architect, Willoughby Fletcher & Associates

Photographed by Sam Lambert in 1967

Bargates in Burton-on-Trent was one of a number of shopping centres built in Britain during the 1960s. Typically for its time, the centre comprised a relatively self-contained precinct containing shops, restaurants and a bowling alley, apparently the first in Burton. Cars were separated from pedestrians, a key tenet of the Modernist approach to urban planning that had its roots in Le Corbusier's city plans of the 1920s. For Le Corbusier, the street was a place of disorder: dangerous, dirty and irrational. Thus, in his (in)famous Plan Voisin of 1925, he proposed demolishing a vast swathe of Paris and replacing it with a series of cruciform towers aligned on a rational grid. The car was glorified as the defining symbol of the personal and social emancipation that could be achieved by technology. Huge motorways would carry traffic at speed, while people could wander freely in the open parkland between the towers.

Realisation of these ideas, particularly in the decades after the Second World War, was usually a world away from Le Corbusier's utopian visions. Old residential streets were swept away in slum clearances, the density on which local urban economies depended was deliberately reduced in the new developments, and motorways were driven through the heart of towns and cities, all in the name of urban renewal. In retrospect, it is no surprise that these kinds of urban intervention caused the orthodox Modernist hold over architecture and planning to begin to loosen. Bargates lasted until 2007 and was subsequently demolished, taking with it the dramatic concrete relief created by the prolific post-war public artist William Mitchell, which is visible here, adorning the building to the left of the frame.

Trinity Square

Gateshead,
Tyne & Wear,
1967

Demolished in
2010

Architect,
Rodney Gordon
for Owen Luder
Partnership

Photographed
by Sam Lambert
in 1967

It is some irony that the new Trinity Square in Gateshead, developed by Tesco and home to one of their gargantuan 'Extra' stores, was nominated in 2014 for the Carbuncle Cup, an annual prize awarded to the ugliest building completed in the UK over the preceding twelve months. The building it replaced, also known as Trinity Square and also a shopping centre (with attached car park), was itself frequently derided as one of the worst eyesores to afflict the north of England. To many, Trinity Square was the archetypal 'concrete monstrosity', a hulking grey mass that dominated Gateshead's skyline and seemed to repel all who looked at it.

The intentions behind the project were, of course, rather different. In 1961, the local council invited developers to propose schemes for what was hoped might become a bustling new town centre. A proposal backed by the E. Alec Colman Group was chosen with the Owen Luder Partnership as architects. In the architectural historian Elain Harwood's words, Luder 'personified the post-war commercial architect, working-class, tough and ambitious'. Concrete was his material of choice, being both economical and allowing for the creation of varied and interesting spaces. Luder would often produce an initial design for a project which was then worked up by others, notably Rodney Gordon, who was responsible for the detailed design of a number of key projects during the 1960s, including Trinity Square.

The scheme consisted of a seven- storey car park with lift and stair towers adjoining a pedestrianised square, with different levels of retail units. While still under construction, Trinity Square appeared as a location in the Michael Caine film *Get Carter!* (1971), whose director, Mike Hodges, was a friend of Gordon's. During the film, Caine's character, the eponymous Jack Carter, who famously sends a rival plummeting to his death from the top of the car park's roof, notes that he is in the process of opening a restaurant there. In reality, the planned roof-top café and club never found a tenant, while the shopping centre as a whole always struggled to compete with other retail destinations. By the mid-1980s it had fallen into terminal decline and it was finally demolished in 2010.

Pimlico Secondary School

Lupus Street, Westminster, London, 1070

Demolished in 2010

Architect, John Bancroft for Greater London Council, Department of Architecture & Civic Design

Unknown photographer, 1971

John Bancroft began working for the LCC schools division in 1957, and was involved in a number of projects that helped to shape the ideas he brought to bear with full force when designing Pimlico Secondary School – one of the last large-scale inner-city comprehensives built by the LCC.

The tight site for a school that was intended to accommodate 1725 pupils required some clever thinking. By the mid-1960s, lifts were already deemed to be out of the question for schools. So Bancroft conceived a building of four storeys, the first of which was sunken into the ground to the level of the basements of the townhouses that had previously occupied the site. The building emerged from this hole in a vast mass of interlocking volumes, overhangs and step-backs, with its glass and concrete materials palette given a clear sense of order through a carefully composed arrangement of angles and planes, which defined the sophisticated arrangement of interior spaces. This complex organisation was intended to bring natural light deep into the building. Unfortunately this feature became one of the building's biggest problems when the air-conditioning machinery was vandalised soon after the school opened. The problem was never properly overcome.

Despite the school developing a reputation in music and the arts, thanks in part to the high-quality facilities that Bancroft had designed, in 1995 Westminster Council proposed redeveloping the site. To some extent this was a consequence of negative attitudes towards the architecture and the values it expressed; the council leader claimed the building was 'entirely without merit and … a significant cause of the difficulties that have faced the school for many years'. But it was also because of the high value of the inner-city site and the money that could be made by allowing a portion of it to be developed for residential use. Despite a spirited campaign led by Bancroft and widely supported by others, including Richard Rogers, the school was demolished in 2010 and replaced under the Labour government's Building Schools for the Future programme.

Park Hill

Sheffield,
1961

Currently
undergoing
extensive
refurbishment,
with the
first phase
completed in
2011

Architect,
Jack Lynn and
Ivor Smith
for Sheffield
Corporation
City Architect's
Department

Photographed
by Reginald
Hugo de Burgh
Galwey in 1964

Looming high on a hill to the east of Sheffield city centre, at first glance Park Hill has the appearance and monumentality of a cliff face. A closer look, however, reveals a building of great thoughtfulness and no small degree of subtlety. Amazingly, the initial design was developed in only six weeks by its young architects, Jack Lynn and Ivor Smith, working for the city architect's department. Despite the speed at which they had to work, Lynn and Smith managed to combine a careful consideration of the particularities of the site with the latest developments in architectural thinking, notably 'streets in the sky', an innovation with which Park Hill has become synonymous.

Streets in the sky had their origins in Le Corbusier's Unité d'habitation apartments in Marseille (1947–52), which had wide access corridors running through the centre of the building. The idea of placing these 'streets' on the outside appeared in the 1951 competition entries for London's Golden Lane estate by Alison and Peter Smithson, and by Jack Lynn himself, working with Gordon Ryder, who would shortly form the practice Ryder and Yates. At Park Hill, as elsewhere, the streets in the sky were intended to recreate the social interactions of the tight-knit working-class communities the estate had replaced – and were even named after former streets. From a practical point of view, thanks to the clever way the blocks increased in height to maintain a level roofline as they stepped down the slope, they also allowed all except the top floors to be accessed from street level. In the estate's early days the streets in the sky were famously used to make deliveries to people's front doors by milk float.

After the utopian optimism of its early years, poor maintenance and social problems, exacerbated by the city's economic woes during the 1980s, led to a deep decline in Park Hill's reputation. Far from providing opportunities for neighbours to interact, the streets in the sky became frequented by muggers.

Amid much controversy, Park Hill received Grade II* listing status in 1998. This was followed by a part-privatisation and regeneration by developer Urban Splash, with the flats reconfigured and the various hues of coloured brick infilling the building's concrete frame replaced with garish anodised aluminium panels.

Few building types embodied the civic values of post-war Britain more than the modern library. And few architects of the era were quite as accomplished at library design as Ahrends, Burton & Koralek (ABK). In fact, the practice was formed after Peter Ahrends, Richard Burton and Paul Koralek won an international competition for a new library at Trinity College, Dublin, in 1960. The Berkeley Library, as it became, was a tour de force of white reinforced concrete, immaculate detailing and an elegant interior arrangement of floors that allowed the building to connect sensitively with its surroundings.

ABK's design for a new library for Redcar in North Yorkshire, produced ten years later, showed how the practice were as adept at working in a structural vocabulary of exposed steel as they were in raw concrete. The use of steel was intended both to reflect and, in a small way, support Redcar's history of steel production. Steel columns held long beams on which the distinctive folded roof profile rested, letting light into the heart of the open space below. Corrugated steel and blue engineering bricks completed a stripped-back, almost industrial materials palette. But while the library was economical in materials, it was hugely generous in its spaces and openness. One of its major innovations was something now taken for granted in library design: the integration of a variety of other amenities, including a café, gallery space and somewhere for children. The clever structure allowed these spaces to be largely continuous, with quiet areas for reading and research located upstairs.

On the whole, Redcar District Library was well liked and well used, but like so many council-owned buildings it suffered from inadequate maintenance. Citing the building's poor condition as well as its lacklustre energy performance (not unusual for buildings of its era), in the late 2000s the council began to work up plans for its demolition and replacement with a multi-use complex. Despite attempts to get the building protected by listing, a campaign which attracted wide support from the architectural profession, and an offer from ABK itself to oversee an inexpensive refurbishment, the library was demolished in 2011.

David Lister
High School

Hull, 1965

Demolished in
2012

Architect,
Lyons, Israel
& Ellis

Unknown
photographer,
1966 and 1969

Although best known for their work during the 1950s and 1960s, the practice that would become Lyons, Israel & Ellis was actually formed by Edward Lyons and Lawrence Israel before the war. In 1947 they were joined by Tom Ellis, whose presence would see the practice quickly emerge as one of the most creative around, attracting young architects including James Stirling, James Gowan and Neave Brown, who would go on to be major figures in their own right. Most of their clients were in the public sector, with the practice working across a number of building types. Education, however, was really where they made their name and were most prolific, completing a total of 25 schools.

In the decades following the war, new schools rose all over the country in response to both the population boom and the fact that so many existing ones had suffered bomb damage. With speed and economy of construction a necessity, there were many innovations in prefabrication, standardisation, procurement – and, of course, design. One of the most famous schools of the era, Alison and Peter Smithson's Hunstanton School in Norfolk (1952–53), combined an innovative plan with a stripped-back aesthetic of steel frame and brick infill.

Hunstanton School was one of the first examples of the 'New Brutalism', a style better known for its manifestations in concrete, which Lyons, Israel & Ellis brought into school design, notably at David Lister High School in Hull. Here, the buildings housing the administration and communal spaces were arranged around the taller teaching blocks, with the concrete structure left raw and exposed, appearing both economical and powerfully sculptural. In its early days David Lister High School was a bastion of progressive teaching practice under headmaster Albert Rowe, but by the late 2000s standards had fallen dramatically. The school was closed in 2012 and demolished soon after.

Red Road Flats

Balornock,
Glasgow, 1969

Final six
point blocks
demolished in
October 2015

Architect,
Sam Bunton &
Associates

Unknown
photographer,
1960

When completed in 1969, the six 31-storey towers of Glasgow's Red Road Flats were among the tallest residential buildings in Europe. Together with the two slightly lower slab blocks, the eight buildings provided 1350 homes for more than 4700 people. This was social housing on a colossal scale, built to alleviate the overcrowding of Glasgow's many slums. In 1966, Edward Clark, convenor of Glasgow Corporation's housing committee, which had commissioned the flats, described to *The Glasgow Herald* how they would offer 'many of our citizens in the Springburn area and other districts who look forward to living in decent surroundings with all the modern amenities that they have so long desired'.

Unusually for the time, the flats were of steel-frame construction, which made extensive fire-proofing with asbestos necessary. However, there was little these precautions could do to prevent a major fire on the twenty-third floor of one of the blocks in 1977, which resulted in the death of a young boy as well as extensive damage. By then popular opinion was already turning against the estate, which was increasingly plagued by crime and anti-social behaviour.

In the 1980s, two of the blocks were deemed no longer fit for families and were transferred for use by students and the YMCA. Despite the introduction around this time of new secure entry systems, a 24-hour concierge and some external recladding, the reputation of the Red Road Flats continued to decline and they became a highly visible symbol of the failures of Glasgow's post-war social housing.

When demolition was first mooted in 2005, the estate was home to significant numbers of asylum seekers, many of whom had fled the war in Kosovo in 1999. Two of the blocks were demolished in 2012 and 2013, with the final ones brought down in October 2015.

Cockenzie
Power Station

Cockenzie and
Port Seton,
Lothian, 1967

Demolished in
2015

Architect,
Robert Matthew
Johnson-
Marshall &
Partners

Photographed
by Henk Snoek
in 1971

For nearly 50 years, the two 149-metre-tall chimneys of Cockenzie Power Station towered over the East Lothian skyline, a landmark of post-war modernity viewable from the heart of historic Edinburgh. The power station's fuel was coal, mined from nearby collieries that had provided Scotland with heat and energy for centuries. When it opened in 1967, Cockenzie represented just the latest stage of this long history.

Although designed by an architect – Robert Matthew of RMJM, one of the leading post-war practices, which he founded with Stirrat Johnson-Marshall in 1956 – Cockenzie's two towers were hard to describe as architecture in the traditional sense. This was functionalism not as architectural philosophy but as pure necessity. Yet there was a distinctly modern

drama, romance even, in the pencil-thin forms, supported by the more obviously Modernist boiler building with its flat roof and clean lines.

Burning coal to produce electricity is, of course, notoriously dirty and polluting, and towards the end of its life Cockenzie was apparently deemed to be the least efficient of all of the UK's power stations in terms of CO_2 emissions per unit of electricity generated. The power station closed in 2008 amid plans to replace it with a more efficient gas-fired power station – still unrealised. The chimneys stood until 2015 when controlled explosions launched the two towers into each other and in just a few seconds erased one of the Scottish landscape's mightiest landmarks and most prominent reminders of the age of coal.

Control Building and Terminal 1, Heathrow Airport

(Originally London Airport), Hounslow, 1955 and 1968

Control Building demolished in 2015; Terminal 1 demolition ongoing

Architect, Sir Frederick Gibberd

Photographed by Bill Toomey in 1955 and Reginald Hugo de Burgh Galwey in 1968

Before the war, Croydon was London's principal civilian airport. But even in those early days of air transportation, it was clear that a larger facility was needed. During the war, the government requisitioned land around an aerodrome near a village called Heath Row to the west of London, ostensibly for military use. By the end of the war, however, the aerodrome was no longer needed and instead it provided the basis for London's new civilian airport. Service at London Airport, as it was then known, began in 1946, with the terminal facilities consisting of no more than tents and marquees.

In its first year, 63,000 passengers passed through the airport. Numbers grew exponentially and by 1951 it was serving very nearly 800,000 annually. Frederick Gibberd was brought in to design new, more permanent terminal facilities. Gibberd's idea was for these to be placed between the two runways, with separate terminals for long- and short-haul flights. The distinctive brick-faced control tower was opened by the Queen in 1955, along with the Queen's Buildings, which constituted the main entrance to the airport. The Europa and then Oceanic terminal buildings then followed (later renamed Terminal 2 and Terminal 3 respectively).

Terminal 1, which opened in 1969, marked the next stage in the airport's development. At the time it was the largest passenger terminal anywhere in the world and incorporated advances – such as moving walkways – that have since become ubiquitous.

With work finally under way to build Terminal 5 at the far end of the runways, in the early 2000s plans were drawn up to replace Terminals 1 and 2 with a single new terminal. Approval came in 2007, with the demolition of old Terminal 2 beginning in 2009. The Control Building survived until 2015, although it had been replaced by a much taller tower in 2007. Terminal 1 closed in 2015 and will be demolished to facilitate the next stage of the new Terminal 2's expansion programme.

Birmingham Central Library

Chamberlain Square, Birmingham, 1974

Demolished in 2016

Architect, John Madin Design Group

Photographed by Sam Lambert in 1974

John Madin's Birmingham Central Library, which until its demolition in 2015 was one the city's most distinctive landmarks, was in fact the third library to stand on the site. Birmingham's first public library opened in 1865, but was badly damaged in a fire fourteen years later and subsequently replaced by a new building which opened in 1882. It was this building, which by the 1960s was far too small to house its collection, that made way for Madin's new library. The foundation stone was laid in 1970, with the library already in use before its formal opening by Prime Minister Harold Wilson in January 1974.

In conceiving the library's distinctive inverted ziggurat form, Madin and project architect John Ericsson looked to work by their contemporaries, Denys Lasdun and Leslie Martin, and to Le Corbusier's influential monastery at La Tourette in the south of France (completed in 1960). Any resemblance to the inverted ziggurat of Boston City Hall in Massachusetts (by Kallman McKinnell & Knowles, 1968) was apparently coincidental, though both buildings take similar approaches to the dramatic expression of civic grandeur in raw concrete.

Working with librarian Bill Taylor, Ericsson cleverly separated the lending and reference libraries, with the former contained in a glazed building that faced an open courtyard and the latter housed in the ziggurat. A central glazed atrium allowed daylight to permeate the reading rooms in the heart of the building, while protecting the collection from excessive light and heat.

Right up to its closure in 2013, Central Library remained one the largest and best used non-national libraries in Europe. Its uncompromising appearance attracted criticism, inevitably from Prince Charles, to whom it looked like 'a place where books are incinerated, not kept'. Nevertheless, this was a building that many local people felt passionate about, and as the plans were put forward by the council for its replacement with a new Library of Birmingham, a campaign was launched to try to get it listed. Despite the recommendations by English Heritage that Central Library should be listed at Grade II, an immunity from listing was granted by Secretary of State Margaret Hodge in 2009. Demolition eventually began in 2016.

Balfron Tower

Rowlett Street, Poplar, London, 1965

Currently undergoing substantial internal alterations

Architect, Ernő Goldfinger

Unknown photographer, 1960

The great concrete slab that rises up next to the busy Blackwall Tunnel approach road is one of the most arresting architectural sights anywhere in London. Balfron Tower's 26 storeys combine a massive, monumental rawness with a geometrical purity conveyed through its rectilinear concrete frame. Distinguishing it from other towers of similar stature is a semi-detached service and lift tower, which, as in Trellick Tower – Balfron's younger, smarter cousin in Kensington – is connected to the main slab at three-storey intervals by thin covered walkways that appear almost to float in mid-air. In a move of supreme elegance, Balfron's architect, the Hungarian émigré Ernő Goldfinger, designed the circulation system so that the front doors for three floors of dwellings all sit on these levels, with doors side by side that lead either up or down to larger dual-aspect flats, or straight across into smaller single-bedroom ones.

With all 146 generously proportioned residences – reached through a marble-lined communal entrance hall – having large balconies, modern kitchens and bathrooms, and access to an underground car park, Balfron was the apogee of forwarding-thinking 1960s social housing. As if to prove the point, Goldfinger famously moved into flat 130 with his wife Ursula Blackwell shortly after the building's completion in 1968, holding a series of champagne receptions for residents to hear what they thought of their new homes.

The national mood was quickly turning against high-rise living, however, and the subsequent reality was inevitably rather different from Goldfinger's utopian optimism. Having been listed in 1996, Balfron is safe from the wrecking ball, though a substantial renovation is currently seeing the building undergo a controversial metamorphosis from social housing to luxury flats marketed to workers in nearby Canary Wharf – a far cry from the social ideals that drove its creation.

The Aylesbury Estate

Walworth, London, 1970

Demolition begun in 2012

Architect, Hans Peter 'Felix' Trenton for London Borough of Southwark, Department of Architecture & Planning

Photographed by Tony Ray-Jones in 1970

On 2 June 1997, Tony Blair delivered his first speech as Prime Minister, not in some leafy suburb but among the vast slab blocks and concrete walkways of one of Britain's largest housing estates: the Aylesbury in south London. The location was carefully chosen for a speech in which Blair famously declared, 'I don't want there to be any forgotten people in the Britain we want to build'. His meaning was twofold: those long ignored by the state would find New Labour far more receptive to their plight than previous administrations, but a life on benefits would be an option for no-one and those able to work would be expected to do so. This was a bargain that went to the core of New Labour's approach to welfare policy, which would have implications for estates and their residents all over the country, not least the Aylesbury.

Covering a huge site between Walworth Road and Old Kent Road, at its height the Aylesbury Estate comprised 2700 homes, housing close to 10,000 people. While in plan the estate is generous with plenty of open spaces, with its extensive use of concrete panels, the Aylesbury is architecturally

uncompromising, sparking controversy from early on. At its opening, Ian Andrews, a Conservative local councillor, said that it was 'a concrete jungle and just not fit for people to live in'. Within a decade, the estate was beset by rough sleepers and drug users taking advantage of the blocks' communal areas, and the familiar problems of infestations and an erratic heating system.

By the 1990s, better security provision and changes to the elevated circulation had improved things considerably. Nevertheless, soon after Blair's visit the local council was given funds for a comprehensive redevelopment of the site. These proposals were overwhelmingly rejected in a ballot of residents in 2001. Despite this opposition, which some residents have continued to voice, four years later the council put forward another scheme for the phased redevelopment of the whole site. Work began in 2010 and is planned to continue in stages until 2032. Today, many of the estate's blocks lie empty behind a high pink fence erected after protestors opposed to the regeneration occupied a number of flats in early 2015.

Centre Point

101 New Oxford Street, London, 1966

Currently undergoing substantial internal alterations

Architect, R. Seifert & Partners

Photographed by Charles Wormald in 1967

Richard Seifert was one of the most prominent – and successful – commercial architects of the post-war era. Having qualified as an architect before the Second World War, he served with the Royal Engineers in India and Burma, eventually reaching the rank of colonel. His practice expanded rapidly during the late 1950s and 1960s as he gained a reputation as an extremely savvy operator who famously appeared to know the planning system better than the planners themselves. Design work was usually left to others in the practice, notably George Marsh.

Seifert was the obvious architect to go to when property developer Harry Hyams acquired a number of plots around St Giles Circus in London in preparation for a large-scale project. Hyams and Seifert hatched a deal with the LCC that gave over some of the site for roads to relieve the heavy traffic congestion, in return for being able to build to the maximum permissible floor area for the whole site, thus allowing Seifert to go much higher than usually possible. In the end he managed to squeeze out

33 storeys for the office tower and eight storeys for the adjoining block containing offices, shops and some housing units. For the tower Marsh conceived an ingenious structural system of pre-cast T-frames, stacked together to form the elevations of the fin-shaped building, which when completed in 1966 was Britain's tallest.

Despite Seifert's clear architectural success, Centre Point, as the building had become known, remained empty until 1975. Hyams calculated that he was better off taking a short-term financial hit and waiting for prices to rise before signing up a sole tenant on a long-term lease. The sight of such a prominent building standing empty naturally provoked stinging criticism. In 1974 Centre Point was even taken over by a group of activists protesting against housing shortages, sparking an association with the otherwise unrelated homelessness charity, also called Centrepoint, founded five years earlier. In this light, it is ironic that the building is now being converted into apartments, albeit ones out of reach for all but the very wealthy.

Robin Hood Gardens

Poplar,
London, 1972

Due to be
demolished in
2016

Architect,
Alison and
Peter Smithson

Photographed
by Tony
Ray-Jones in
1970

Although the LCC had its own in-house architects' department, on occasion it also commissioned other architects. Among the most notable were Alison and Peter Smithson. While they built relatively little, the husband-and-wife duo had an international reputation, garnered largely through their membership of Team X, which in 1959 had helped to precipitate the dissolution of C.I.A.M. (Congrès International d'Architecture Moderne), the association of architects that aimed to spread Modernist ideas around the world. In Britain the Smithsons' fame extended from their membership of the influential Independent Group, their appearance in the seminal exhibition *This is Tomorrow* held at the Whitechapel Art Gallery in 1956, to their role as leading figures of the 'New Brutalism' movement – a radical attempt at reinvigorating architectural Modernism by connecting it to the realities of everyday life.

Brutalism's most recognisable characteristic was its insistence on leaving materials in their raw, unfinished state. But in terms of how a building actually functioned, its most important innovation in housing design was 'streets in the sky'. The Smithsons had pioneered the idea in their 1952 competition

entry for London's Golden Lane estate, and the concept had been realised in other developments, notably Sheffield's Park Hill. However, Robin Hood Gardens was the Smithsons' first opportunity to put the idea into practice. It is perhaps for this reason that the streets in the sky at Robin Hood Gardens have an unmistakable bravura: thanks to a clever structural solution that eliminated the need for vertical supports, they appear as uninterrupted bands encircling the two pincer-like slab blocks that turn in towards each other around a raised garden. The geometrical composition of the façades ensured the external legibility of the interior configuration of flats and maisonettes, while imbuing the buildings with a sculptural force not unlike that found in the work of one of the Smithsons' heroes, the English Baroque architect, John Vanbrugh.

Despite the Smithsons' idealism, there was little their building could do to alleviate the social problems and poverty that plagued the area. Lack of maintenance coupled with design faults has seen Robin Hood Gardens fall into a state of substantial disrepair and, despite passionate campaigns for it to be listed, demolition is likely to begin in 2016.

Elephant and Castle Shopping Centre

Southwark, London, 1965

Due to be demolished in the next two years

Architect, Boissevain & Osmond

Photographed by Peter Baistow in 1965

The area of inner south London around Elephant and Castle was devastated during the Blitz. Soon after the war, a series of comprehensive redevelopment plans were proposed for rebuilding the area, allowing the intersection of major roads leading to Westminster, Waterloo, Blackfriars and London Bridge to regain its pre-war title of the 'Piccadilly Circus of South London'.

The shopping centre derives from an open competition launched by the LCC in 1959. The winning entry by architects Boissevain & Osmond working for the developer Willetts Group consists of a piazza below street level into which is sunk a three-storey podium, originally intended to contain space for more than one hundred shops, underground car parks, a banqueting suite, restaurants, a bowling alley and two pubs. Above the whole composition stands Hannibal House – an eleven-storey office block in a stripped-back International Style. The concept owed much to American precedents in creating a safe and regulated world of shopping, separated from the disorder of the surrounding city. It was one of the first shopping centres to be built in Britain and at the time of its completion was claimed to be one of the largest in Europe.

Despite the optimism that surrounded the project in its early stages, budget restrictions during construction ensured that the shopping centre as built was meaner in both finish and layout than originally intended. On its opening in 1965, less than half the shops were occupied and despite several attempts at rebranding and refitting, including painting the whole building hot pink in the 1990s, the centre has always been deemed a failure. Although frequently described as an eyesore and often appearing in lists of London's ugliest buildings, in recent years it has provided relatively affordable space for a more diverse range of shops than is found in other centres, especially in the market in the sunken piazza. The shopping centre is scheduled to be demolished in the next few years as part of a wider redevelopment of Elephant and Castle.

Fairfax Street Sports Centre

Coventry, 1966, extension opened in 1977

Under substantial threat from redevelopment

Architect, Coventry City Architect's Department

Unknown photographer and Bill Toomey, 1966

The destruction of Coventry's medieval city centre by enemy bombing was one of the saddest architectural losses of the Second World War. It was matched only by the firestorms inflicted on the German city of Dresden, with the shared trauma seeing the two cities becoming twinned in 1959. In light of its wartime devastation, it is often forgotten that Coventry's character had already begun to change before the war with the growth of the car industry and the presence of munitions factories developed during the First World War. Its importance as a manufacturing centre was of course part of the reason why the city was such a key target.

Proposals for modernising the city were under discussion before the war, and as early as 1941 the city's architect, Donald Gibson, had drawn up a comprehensive scheme for rebuilding the centre. Gibson's plan comprised an inner ring road which would contain various semi-discrete precincts, with space allocated for a huge new shopping centre, for Basil Spence's celebrated cathedral to be built alongside the preserved ruins of the old medieval one, and for a new sports and swimming centre, which eventually opened in 1966.

An international-standard pool, lit by three-storey glass walls, was arranged under a soaring W-shaped roof, with two further pools providing space for learners and social swimmers. Although the large pool could accommodate a thousand spectators, the centre was always designed primarily for community use rather than for a major sports event. 'The Elephant' extension was added in 1977, standing astride Cox Street and reached by an elevated walkway.

The main building is shortly due to close with the council working on a replacement leisure-centre complex on New Union Street. While in a state of some disrepair, the building is listed, though this does not include 'The Elephant' extension, raising serious questions about the fate of this charmingly idiosyncratic local landmark.

St Peter's Seminary

Cardross,
Dunbartonshire,
1966

Closed in 1980;
current plans
envisage
partial
restoration

Architect,
Gillespie,
Kidd & Coia

Photographed
by Studio Brett
in 1960

In a wood outside the village of Cardross, which overlooks the River Clyde as it makes its way out to sea, lies one of the great ruins of the modern age: St Peter's Roman Catholic Seminary. Although widely acknowledged as one of Scotland's Modernist masterpieces, the seminary has spent more time abandoned than actually in use. It was designed by Andy MacMillan and Isi Metzstein of Gillespie, Kidd & Coia as a training centre for Catholic priests. However, by the time it was completed the Second Vatican Council had decreed that priests should no longer be trained in seclusion but in the communities they would ultimately serve, rendering the new facility redundant. The seminary continued to function until 1980, after which the building housed a drug rehabilitation centre before being finally abandoned in 1990 and soon falling into ruin.

MacMillan and Metzstein's sources ranged from the Modernist touchstones of Frank Lloyd Wright and Le Corbusier to Scotland's own Charles Rennie Mackintosh and the heavy Baronial architecture that rose across the country during the seventeenth century. Indeed, their buildings at Cardross were originally planned around a nineteenth-century Baronial Revival mansion (demolished after a fire in 1995). An L-shaped plan separated out the teaching block from the refectory, chapel and bedrooms, which were arranged in a dramatic stepped section in the long range running east to west. Bold cantilevers extended the building into the landscape, while gently filtering the light entering the chapel that lay at the heart of the whole composition. In its stripped-back roughness of form and surface, the building clearly looked to Le Corbusier's monastery at La Tourette (1956–60), yet MacMillan and Metszein brought a passion and sculptural drama that was all theirs.

For all its apparent robustness, the seminary suffered from leaks from early on, so when it was abandoned the decay quickly spread and it now lies roofless and open to the elements. Plans are, however, afoot to re-roof and partially refurbish the building as a venue for concerts, performances and the arts. Fittingly, the proposals would not see the building restored, just made safe and habitable, thus retaining the ruined quality that has caught the imagination of so many over the last three decades.

Endnotes

1 Charles Jencks, *The Language of Post-Modern Architecture*, London, 1977, p. 9.

2 Examples include work by architects such as Neave Brown, whose Alexandra Road (properly the Alexandra and Ainsworth estate, completed in 1978) in north London made use of a complex, ziggurat-like section that ensured every home had its own front door and private external space. At Cressingham Gardens (also 1978), an estate in south London by Lambeth Borough Architects led by Ted Hollamby, there a number of different sizes of residence were arranged around a series of paths and a 'village green'.

3 The speech was delivered on 30 May 1984 at Hampton Court Palace at an event intended to mark the 150th anniversary of the RIBA and the awarding of the RIBA Gold Medal to the Indian architect Charles Correa.

4 David Cameron, 'I've put the bulldozing of sink estates at the heart of turnaround Britain', *The Sunday Times*, 10 January 2016.

5 One of the most vocal is the campaign to prevent the decanting of tenants and leaseholders from the Aylesbury Estate in south London.

6 William Beveridge, *Social Insurance and Allied Services*, London, 1942.

7 For background, see Mary Banham and Bevis Hillier (eds), *A Tonic to the Nation: The Festival of Britain 1951*, London, 1976.

8 The idea for a 'live' exhibition of architecture came from Frederick Gibberd, who felt strongly that the public would be far more inspired by a real, functioning housing estate than by drawings and models. With time short, what became the Lansbury Estate in Poplar, which was already under way, was chosen as the site. Although in some ways typical of LCC planning and design of the time, the involvement of the Festival did see a greater range of architects incorporated in the Lansbury Estate than elsewhere. They included Geoffrey Jellicoe, Norman & Dawbarn and Bridgwater & Shepheard.

9 The epithet was coined by the critic Reyner Banham in a seminal essay published in *Architectural Review* in December 1955 and then developed in his book *The New Brutalism: Ethic or Aesthetic?*, London, 1966.

10 Ian Nairn, 'Outrage', a special edition of *Architectural Review*, vol. 117, no. 702, June 1955.

11 In the case of the last, a campaign led by local people and supporters from outside succeeded in saving the historic market. The victory was to play an important part in the growing conservation movement.

12 *Architecture at the Crossroads*, episode 1, 'Doubt and Reassessment', first shown 12 January 1986 (extract is at 9.03).

13 The crisis was the result of an embargo on oil exports imposed by the Organization of Arab Petroleum Exporting Countries in reaction to Western support for Israel in the Yom Kippur war with Egypt. Among the effects in Britain were fuel shortages and rocketing inflation.

14 Hayek's most famous and influential work is *The Road to Serfdom*, first published in 1944.

15 Margaret Thatcher was greatly influenced by Coleman's work and invited her to 10 Downing Street to discuss it. Thatcher subsequently set up a programme to put her recommendations into practice. More broadly, Coleman's evidence of the apparent practical failures of social housing provided fertile ground for the dismantling of the ideologies on which its creation had rested. For more, see 'Nicholas Boys Smith and James Wildblood interview Prof Alice Coleman, housing visionary', *Conservative Home*, 11 July 2014: http://www.conservativehome.com/localgovernment/2014/07/nicholas-boys-smith-and-james-wildblood-interview-with-professor-alice-coleman.html

16 Kingsley Amis, 'Sod the Public – A Consumer's Guide', *The Spectator*, 18 October 1985: http://archive.spectator.co.uk/article/19th-october-1985/9/sod-the-public-a-consumers-guide

17 Prominent critics of modern architecture included the philosopher Roger Scruton, architectural historian David Watkin, and playwright Peter Shaffer, whose play *Lettice and Lovage* (1988) sees two friends brought together over their shared hatred of modern architecture.

18 The Hayward Gallery, which opened in 1968, was designed by Dennis Crompton, Warren Chalk and Ron Herron, working for the LCC. All three were members of the avant-garde group Archigram. The Queen Elizabeth Hall and Purcell Room were designed by a separate LCC team and opened in 1967.

19 Critics of PFI have noted that rather than reducing costs through the efficiencies believed to come with private capital, it has actually increased them. Given the way that so many hospitals in particular have been crippled by debt repayments that will continue for decades, they probably have a point. That said, the need for investment was clear. Despite the cost, New Labour's transformation of Britain's hospital and school building stock has on the whole been for the better, with many tired and neglected post-war buildings replaced by new facilities. See Robert Mendick, Laura Donnelly and Ashley Kirk, 'The PFI hospitals costing NHS £2bn every year', *The Daily Telegraph*, 18 July 2015: http://www.telegraph.co.uk/news/nhs/11748960/The-PFI-hospitals-costing-NHS-2bn-every-year.html

20 In 2014/15, the total Housing Benefit bill was £27 billion. See: http://visual.ons.gov.uk/welfare-spending/. It is unclear how much of this is spent on subsidising rents of homes that were once owned by the state.

21 See comments by Meades in an event on 'Architectural Ethics' organised by the Royal Academy of Arts on 9 November 2015. The recording is available at https://www.royalacademy.org.uk/article/podcast-architecture-and-freedom-season (his comments are at 31.14).

22 This was discussed in Crinson's lecture 'Brutalism – from New to Neo', at Birkbeck, University of London, on 19 May 2016: http://www.bbk.ac.uk/assc/2016/03/21/prof-mark-crinson-talk-brutalism-from-new-to-neo/

23 Examples include the Twitter account The Brutal House @ BrutalHouse and the blog: fuckyeahbrutalism.tumblr.com

24 Early advocates for Brutalism included Jonathan Meades and Stephen Bayley. See for example the latter's BBC programme for the *Building Sights* series on Ernő Goldfinger's Alexander Fleming House in London: http://www.bbc.co.uk/programmes/p01rqpwx

25 All three were members of the influential Independent Group, which also included architects Alison and Peter Smithson. The group, which first met in 1952, sought to challenge the elites of the cultural establishment by drawing from mass culture and making frequent use of 'found' objects in their work. The group came to widespread attention with the seminal exhibition *This is Tomorrow* held at the Whitechapel Gallery in 1956.

26 One of the best known is the work *Seizure* (2008 and 2013) for which the artist Roger Hiorns lined the interior of a condemned Peckham council flat with brilliant blue copper-sulphate crystals. The work was subsequently painstakingly extracted and now sits in a purpose-built concrete block in Yorkshire Sculpture Park. It invites multiple interpretations: for some, it is about making beauty out of the mundane; for others, it functions almost as a protest against the political and economic forces driving demolition, particularly of housing.

Further Reading

Lawrence Alloway, David Lewis and Reyner Banham, *This is Tomorrow* (facsimile of original 1956 exhibition catalogue), London, 2010

Trevor Dannatt, *Modern Architecture in Britain*, London, 1959

Ian Nairn, *Modern Buildings in Britain*, London, 1964

Reyner Banham, *The New Brutalism: Ethic or Aesthetic?*, London, 1966

Ian Nairn, *Britain: Changing Towns*, London, 1967 (new edition published as Owen Hatherley (ed.), *Nairn''s Towns*, London, 2013)

Robert Maxwell, *New British Architecture*, London, 1972

Charles Jencks, *Modern Movements in Architecture*, Harmondsworth, 1973

Mary Banham and Bevis Hillier (eds), *A Tonic to the Nation: The Festival of Britain 1951*, London, 1976

Charles Jencks, *The Language of Post-Modern Architecture*, London, 1977 (reissued as *The New Paradigm in Architecture: The Language of Post-Modernism*, New Haven and London, 2002)

James Dunnett, Gavin Stamp, Charlotte Perriand, *Ernő Goldfinger: Works 1*, London, 1983

Alice M. Coleman, *Utopia on Trial: Vision and Reality in Planned Housing*, London, 1985

Charles, Prince of Wales, *A Vision of Britain: A Personal View of Architecture*, New York and London, 1989

David Robbins (ed.), *The Independent Group: Postwar Britain and the Aesthetics of Plenty*, Cambridge, Mass., 1990

John Allan, *Berthold Lubetkin: Architecture and the Tradition of Progress*, London, 1992

Miles Glendinning and Stefan Muthesius, *Tower Block: Modern Public Housing in England, Scotland, Wales, and Northern Ireland*, New Haven and London, 1994

Anne Massey, *The Independent Group: Modernism and Mass Culture in Britain, 1949–59*, Manchester, 1996

Robert Elwall, *Building a Better Tomorrow*, Hoboken, N.J., 2000

Owen Hatherley, *Militant Modernism*, Alresford, 2009

Owen Hatherley, *A Guide to the New Ruins of Great Britain*, London and New York, 2010

Barry Turner, *Beacon for Change: How the 1951 Festival of Britain Shaped the Modern Age*, London, 2011

Lynsey Hanley, *Estates: An Intimate History*, London, 2012

Jonathan Meades, *Museum Without Walls*, London, 2012

John Grindrod, *Concretopia: A Journey Around the Rebuilding of Postwar Britain*, London, 2014

Elain Harwood, *Space, Hope, and Brutalism: English Architecture, 1945-1975*, New Haven and London, 2015

Elain Harwood, *England: Post-War Listed Buildings*, 3rd edition, London, 2015

Barnabas Calder, *Raw Concrete: The Beauty of Brutalism*, London, 2016

Photographic Acknowledgements

Index